NATIVE AMERICAN TESTIMONY

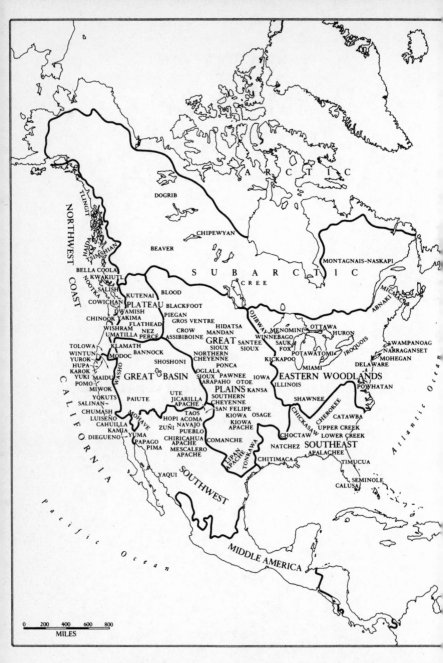

Native American tribes and culture areas, circa 1650. (BERNHARD H. WAGNER)

NATIVE AMERICAN TESTIMONY

An Anthology
of Indian and White Relations

First Encounter to Dispossession

PREFACE BY VINE DELORIA, JR.

Edited by Peter Nabokov

R. REGINALD
The Borgo Press
San Bernardino, California □ MCMXIII

A hardcover edition of this book was published by Thomas Y. Crowell Company.

First HARPER PAPERBACK edition published 1979.

Library of Congress Cataloging in Publication Data
Main entry under title:

Native American testimony.
  (Harper torchbooks)
  Reprint. Originally published: New York: Crowell, c1978.
  Bibliography: p.
  Includes index.
  Summary: A collection of documents in which Native Americans describe their responses to the explorers, traders, missionaries, settlers, and government diplomats and soldiers seeking dominion over their ancient homeland.
  1. Indians of North America—Government relations—Sources. 2. Indians of North America—History—Sources.
  [1. Indians of North America—History—sources.
  2. Indians of North America—Government relations—Sources] I. Nabokov, Peter.
[E93.N29 1984]   970.004'97   84-48050
ISBN 0-06-131993-7 (pbk.)

92 93 94 95 MPC 15 14 13 12 11 10 9 8

Grateful acknowledgment is made to the following for permission to reprint material copyrighted or controlled by them:

ACADEMY OF AMERICAN FRANCISCAN HISTORY for "The Freedom to Work" from *Indian Life and Customs at Mission San Luis Rey* by Pablo Tac. Edited and translated with a historical introduction by Minna and Gordon Hewes (1958).

AMERICAN FOLKLORE SOCIETY for "Black Hawk Stands Alone" from "Black-Hawk War" by William Jones. *Journal of American Folklore*, 24:235–237, 1911; for "Buttocks Bags and Green Coffee Bread" from "Rations" by M. E. Opler, *Memoirs of the American Folklore Society*, Vol. XXXI, p. 362–363, 1938; for "Before They Got Thick" from "The White People Who Came in a Boat" by M. E. Opler, *Memoirs of the American Folklore Society*, Vol. XXXVI, pp. 283–284, 1940.

THE BANCROFT LIBRARY, University of California, Berkeley, for "Janitin Is Named Jésus" excerpted from "Testimonio de Janitil" from "*Apuntes Historicos de la Baja California*" by Manuel C. Roja.

CALIFORNIA HISTORICAL SOCIETY for "White Rabbit Got Lotsa Everything" from *Out of the Past: A True Indian Story*, told by Lucy Young to Edith V. A. Murphey, *California Historical Society Quarterly*, Vol. XX, No. 4, Dec. 1941; and for "Blood Scattered like Water" from *The Stone and Kelsey "Massacre" on the Shores of Clear Lake in 1849*, *The Indian Viewpoint*, California Historical Society Quarterly, Vol. XI, No. 3, Sept. 1932.

THOMAS Y. CROWELL COMPANY, INC., for "I Hid Myself and Watched," part one (Pretty Shield) from *Pretty Shield: Medicine Woman of the Crows* (originally *Red Mother*) by Frank B. Linderman (John Day Company). Copyright 1932 by Frank B. Linderman, renewed 1960 by Norma Waller, Verne Linderman and Wilda Linderman.

And for "The Buffalo Go" from *American Indian Mythology* by Alice Marriott and Carol K. Rachlin. Copyright 1968 by Alice Marriott and Carol K. Rachlin.

DOVER PUBLICATIONS, INC., for "Always Give Blessings and Be Thankful" from *Jim Whitewolf: The Life of a Kiowa Apache Indian* by Charles S. Brant, Dover Publications, Inc., New York, 1969.

HARVARD UNIVERSITY PRESS for part 2 (Jaime) of "I Hid Myself and Watched" from *The Navaho Door: An Introduction to Navaho Life* by Alexander Leighton and Dorothea Leighton, Harvard University Press, 1944.

HOUGHTON MIFFLIN COMPANY for "A Wish" from *Apauk: Caller of Buffalo* by James Willard Schultz, Houghton Mifflin Company, 1915; and for "Corralling the Navajo" from *The Navajo Indians* by Dane and Mary R. Coolidge, Houghton Mifflin Company, 1930.

HUDSON'S BAY COMPANY and JUNE HELM for "The Bewitched Pale Man" from "Got the Hudson's Bay Man's Mind" in *Tales from the Dogribs* by June Helm, *Beaver Magazine, Autumn, 1966.*

HUDSON'S BAY RECORD SOCIETY, Winnipeg, Canada, for "Give Us Good Goods" from *Isham's Observations and Notes 1743–49*. London: Hudson's Bay Record Society, Volume XII, 1949.

INDIANA HISTORICAL SOCIETY for "Our Very Good Friend Kirk" from *Letter Book of the Indian Agency at Fort Wayne 1809–1815*, edited by Gayle Thornbrough. Copyright Indiana Historical Society, 1961.

MCGRAW-HILL RYERSON LIMITED for "Visitors from Heaven" from *Legends of My People: The Great Ojibway* by Norval Morriseau, edited by Selwyn Dewdney. Copyright © The Ryerson Press, 1965. Reprinted by permission of McGraw-Hill Ryerson Ltd.

THE JOHN G. NEIHARDT TRUST for "The Spider's Web" from *Black Elk Speaks* by John G. Neihardt, copyright John G. Neihardt 1932, 1961. University of Nebraska Press, 1961.

NEW YORK MUSEUM OF THE AMERICAN INDIAN, HEYE FOUNDATION, for "Plenty Coups Travels to Washington" from the unpublished manuscript *A Crow Miscellany* by William Wildschut.

SHERIDAN HOUSE, INC., for "No Dawn to the East" from *Red Man's Reservations* by Clark Wissler. Copyright 1938 by Clark Wissler, copyright renewed 1966 by Mary V. Wissler. Introduction copyright 1971 by The Macmillan Company.

STACKPOLE BOOKS for "Geronimo Puts Down the Gun" from *I Fought With Geronimo* by Jason Betzinez with Wilbur Sturtevant Nye, Stackpole Company, 1959.

STATE HISTORICAL SOCIETY OF NORTH DAKOTA for "Gone Forever" from James E. Sperry, Editor, *Waheenee: An Indian Girl's Story Told By Herself to Gilbert L. Wilson, North Dakota History*, 38, No. 1 & 2 (Winter/Spring, 1971), pp. 175–176. All rights reserved.

SOL TAX and the UNIVERSITY OF CHICAGO for "A Good Indian's Dilemma" from *Being a Mesquakie Indian* by Lisa Redfield Peattie, University of Chicago, 1950.

CHARLES C. THOMAS, PUBLISHER, for "Take Care of Me" from *Broken Peace Pipes* by Irwin M. Peithman, foreword by Loren Taylor, published by Charles C. Thomas, Publisher, Springfield, 1964.

UNIVERSITY OF CALIFORNIA PRESS for "A Shaman Obeys" from "The Language of the Salinan Indians" by J. Alden Mason, *Publications in American Archeology and Ethnology,* Vol. 14, No. 1, University of California Publications, 1918. Published in 1918 by the Regents of the University of California.

UNIVERSITY OF NEW MEXICO PRESS for "Burn the Temples, Break Up the Bells" from *Revolt of the Pueblo Indians of New Mexico and Otermin's Attempted Reconquest 1608–1682,* by Charles Wilson Hackett, O. C. Shelby, translator. Volume IX, Coronado Historical Series, University of New Mexico Press, 1942.

UNIVERSITY OF OKLAHOMA PRESS for "A Different Kind of Man" from *The Assiniboines: From the Accounts of the Old Ones Told to First Boy (James Larpenteur Long),* edited and with an Introduction by Michael Stephen Kennedy. New edition copyright 1961 by the University of Oklahoma Press. And for "If I Could See This Thing" from *Life of George Bent: Written from His Letters* by George E. Hyde, edited by Savoie Lottinville. Copyright 1968 by the University of Oklahoma Press.

CONTENTS

Preface   *ix*
Foreword   *xiii*

PREMONITIONS AND PROPHECIES   1

1 He Will Use Any Means to Get What He Wants
      (*Dan Katchongva, Hopi*)   5
2 White Rabbit Got Lotsa Everything
      (*Lucy Young, Wintun*)   6
3 Visitors from Heaven
      (*Norval Morriseau, Ojibway*)   10
4 Thunder's Dream Comes True
      (*Black Hawk, Sauk*)   12
5 Easy Life of the Gray-Eyed
      (*James Paytiamo, Acoma Pueblo*)   14
6 The Spider's Web
      (*Black Elk, Oglala Sioux*)   16

FACE TO FACE   19

1 Their Wondrous Works and Ways
      (*Charles Alexander Eastman, Santee Sioux*)   23
2 Before They Got Thick
      (*Percy Bigmouth, Lipan Apache*)   26
3 Silmoodawa Gives a Complete Performance
      (*Anonymous, Micmac*)   28
4 A Different Kind of Man
      (*First Boy, Assiniboine*)   30
5 I Hid Myself and Watched
      (*Pretty Shield, Crow; and Jaime, Navajo*)   33

EXCHANGE BETWEEN WORLDS   37

1 Thunder, Dizzying Liquid, and Cups That Do Not
      Grow (*Waioskasit, Menomini*)   42

2 Keep Your Presents (*Curly Chief, Pawnee*)   45

3 Give Us Good Goods (*Anonymous, Tribe unknown*)   47

4 You Rot the Guts of Our Young Men
    (*King Haglar, Catawba*)   48

5 Some Strange Animal (*Wolf Calf, Piegan*)   49

6 Buttocks Bags and Green Coffee Bread
    (*Anonymous, Jicarilla Apache*)   53

7 The Bewitched Pale Man (*Vital Thomas, Dogrib*)   56

BEARERS OF THE CROSS   59

1 Burn the Temples, Break Up the Bells
    (*Pedro Naranjo, San Felipe Pueblo*)   65

2 A Good Indian's Dilemma (*Anonymous, Fox*)   68

3 We Never Quarrel About Religion
    (*Red Jacket, Iroquois*)   69

4 Janitin Is Named *Jesús* (*Janitin, Kamia*)   70

5 The Freedom to Work (*Pablo Tac, Luiseño*)   73

6 A Shaman Obeys (*Pedro Encinales, Salinan*)   77

7 Always Give Blessings and Be Thankful
    (*Jim Whitewolf, Kiowa Apache*)   78

LIVING BESIDE EACH OTHER   83

1 Remove the Cause of Our Uneasiness
    (*Wahunsonacock, Powhatan Confederacy*)   87

2 Mary Jemison Becomes an Iroquois
    (*Mary Jemison, Iroquois*)   89

3 Our Very Good Friend Kirk
    (*The Old Snake, et al., Shawnee*)   96

4 The Frenchman Dreams Himself Home
    (*Anonymous, Winnebago*)   98

5 Incident at Boyer Creek (*Anonymous, Omaha*)   101

6 If I Could See This Thing
    (*George Bent, Southern Cheyenne*)   105

7 All Things Are Connected (*Seattle, Dwamish*)   107

THE LONG RESISTANCE   111

1 We Must Be United (*Tecumseh, Shawnee*)   118

2   Black Hawk Stands Alone (*William Jones, Fox*)   121
3   Blood Scattered like Water (*William Benson, Pomo*)   125
4   Young Men, Go Out and Fight Them
      (*Wooden Leg, Northern Cheyenne*)   132
5   Geronimo Puts Down the Gun
      (*Jason Betzinez, Southern Chiricahua Apache*)   139

THE TREATY TRAIL   147

1   Let Us Examine the Facts (*Corn Tassel, Cherokee*)   152
2   Osceola Determined (*Osceola, et al., Seminole*)   155
3   My Son, Stop Your Ears (*Chief Joseph, Nez Percé*)   162
4   We Are Not Children (*Medicine Horse, et al., Otoe*)   168
5   Plenty Coups Travels to Washington
      (*Plenty Coups, Crow*)   176

EXILES IN THEIR OWN LAND   183

1   Plea from the Chickasaw (*Levi Colbert, et al., Chickasaw*)   190
2   Tushpa Crosses the Mississippi
      (*James Culberson, Choctaw*)   191
3   Corralling the Navajo (*Chester Arthur, Navajo*)   197
4   The Uprooted Winnebago (*Little Hill, Winnebago*)   203
5   Standing Bear's Odyssey (*Standing Bear, Ponca*)   207

THE NATION'S HOOP IS BROKEN AND SCATTERED   215

1   The Buffalo Go (*Old Lady Horse, Kiowa*)   220
2   Take Care of Me (*Wild Cat, Seminole*)   222
3   I Am Alone (*Cochise, Chiricahua Apache*)   222
4   I Have Spoken (*Crazy Horse, Oglala Sioux*)   225
5   I Want to Look for My Children
      (*Chief Joseph, Nez Percé*)   227
6   No Dawn to the East (*Anonymous, Tribe unknown*)   228
7   Gone Forever (*Buffalo Bird Woman, Hidatsa*)   229
8   This Awful Loneliness (*Anonymous, Omaha*)   231
9   A Wish (*Flint Knife, Blackfoot*)   232

NOTES ON SOURCES   233
INDEX   239

PREFACE

Arnold Toynbee once remarked that reading world history as it is presently structured is akin to receiving a map of the Mediterranean region and being informed that it represents a chart of the entire planet. American history suffers something of the same parochial flavor. Indians seem to represent the mysterious, unfathomable dimension of the unknown that first frightened the settlers and which transformed itself time and again in each generation to produce that unarticulated fear of the unknown which has characterized much of American history. Standard textbooks and histories concern themselves with the arrangement of historical artifacts—the dates, policies, movements, and institutions which mark the progress of human transformation of the North American continent. Anthologies, for the most part, attempt to illustrate a general theme of the conflicting values that characterized the settlement of America. The missing dimension in our knowledge is the informality of human experience, which colors all our decisions and plays an intimate and influential role in the historical experiences of our species.

Peter Nabokov attempts to move beyond the impasse of his-

torical knowledge by bringing two themes together, thus allow-
ing the traditionally articulated conflict of the races to become
an underlying context within which actual people take part in
and respond to actual events. This method of understanding
history, comparable in many respects to earlier efforts by such
people as Bernard De Voto, imprints memorable events and
personalities on the reader, outside the sort of sterile academic
setting that comands a narrow interpretation of the data. Instead
of the usual process of reading to gain comprehension, the reader
of this anthology will find him or herself engaged in historical
experiences in which the trivial becomes meaningful and the
pompous event finds itself reduced to a human dimension. Life
produces such anomalies, and it is only as we are taught to arrange
experiences in an ascending order of abstractions that we come
to believe otherwise.

Events should really be classified according to their memorable
quality rather than as consecutive aspects of a larger theme. Until
we allow our emotions to dominate our thinking processes, we
cannot actually enter into an understanding of what makes us
human. The selections in this collection bring together occasions
during which we can transcend the limitations of time and space
and participate in the meaning of life as others who have come
before us have known it. Thus the joy and tragedy of the past
enable us to renew the clouded but intense vision of our own
lives; as we walk with our ancestors through the incidents of the
past, we come to a realization of the underlying meaning of
human activities. Some of the selections found here are not unusual in any sense; if we evaluate human expression by its power
to suggest a reality beyond our senses, they record in a few instances events of the most minor importance. Yet these same
incidents, placed within the proper context, reveal the common
condition we share with all previous generations. They remind us

that while we may *misunderstand, we do not misexperience*, and that our fundamental error is our tendency to divide experiences and classify them and label the product *understanding*.

The dilemma of our species is always to be placed between the plateau of wisdom and the desert of ignorance, with mountains of experience to be traversed. Perhaps the outstanding impression which these selections leave with the reader is the very limited scope of awareness that is available to us during any generation. Had the Indians recognized the tremendous gulf in values and world view that separated them from the settlers, could they have acted with sufficient wisdom and craft to preserve a bit of their homelands untouched? Could the settlers have transcended the greed and fanaticism generated by visions of a land rich beyond comprehension to produce a more relaxed, orderly, and generous exploitation of the lands and peoples of North America? These questions, as well as many others, will remain when the last page has been read, the last witness called to testify to the events of our history. Today our problems seem insurmountable, and we find ourselves in nearly every circumstance standing with the personalities of the past, exulting and mourning, but always incapable of achieving a full understanding of our situation. History thus calls us to share, not to render judgments.

Nabokov bids us embark on a historical journey fraught with the unexpected but possessing the substance which we recognize in our own lives. It seems suitable that we are called upon to perform a task of cooperative trailblazing with Nabokov, that we become participants rather than observers. For in reading these vignettes of the past, comparable in many ways to the disjointed and varied lives we live today, we face a task similar to the demands of living, a task we too often shirk. Like the confusion into which we are thrust in our own lives, these nuggets of history require us both to experience and to bring order to our experiences. For the discerning reader, then, this anthology provides more than entertainment or information; it furnishes opportunities for accumulating insights on the meaning of life.

The sole requirement for reading and enjoying this collection is that the reader discard presumptions and preconceptions and immerse the soul in the richness of the human condition. Provocations of emotion are much superior to provocations of the mind alone, and these selections are designed to burst sterile barriers of communication and lead the reader through the twists and turns of human life. The assumption that one party or the other was fated to arrive at their present condition eliminates any possibility of understanding how events occurred and what people felt in the immediate situation and upon later reflection. The skillful balancing of selections here enables one to move along the line of emotions and participate in the grandeur which has made the story of North America among the most exciting episodes of human history. I hope the reader will enjoy this dimension of the book among all others.

Vine Deloria, Jr.
Golden, Colorado

FOREWORD

In this documentary chronicle of Indian and white relations, I have tried to illuminate key historical issues through accounts of both famous and little-known events. When my research turned up a significant number of Indian-spoken or written accounts that shared an underlying point of view, my next step was to choose the selection which expressed it most intimately, dramatically, and persuasively.

Here we glimpse how native peoples faced the conditions of the moment—often crisis conditions—and how they interpreted them afterward. Yet we should not forget that while the American history we study in schoolbooks was being made, another kind of history was taking place; not the chronicle of Indian and white relations, but the internal history of Indian communities, which began long before the arrival of the white man and which, some maintain, will survive long after he is gone. Although the white presence increasingly came to preoccupy Native Americans, many purely Indian personalities, concerns, and events have gone largely unrecorded in written works. Often that is the history the tribes still cherish most.

What we have here are those instances when Indians turned from their private worlds to interact with a new culture, one that could hardly have been more different or more threatening. Sometimes edged with anger or subtle irony, but astonishingly understated and free of corrosive hate, these stories, speeches, and memories stand for countless Native American testimonies that will never be heard.

Peter Nabokov
Pacific Grove, California

PREMONITIONS
AND PROPHECIES

Before the coming of the white man, bronze-skinned men and women from northern Asia had been exploring and settling the Americas for anywhere from ten to fifty thousand years, according to archaeological estimates. They almost certainly began by trekking in small bands from Siberia to Alaska, across a land bridge spanning what is now the Bering Strait. By the fifteenth century their descendants had spread southward to populate both continents.

When Christopher Columbus came ashore in the Bahamas, North America alone was home for an estimated two to ten million people. The Spanish admiral, believing he had found the long-sought western passage to the Asian mainland, made the notorious error of dubbing them "Indians." By then these Native American peoples had developed some three hundred distinct cultures and spoke over two hundred different languages. In North America their numbers were most concentrated along the coastal strip that is now California—about fifty-six people every fifty square miles. The Southwest was a second major population center—nearly fourteen inhabitants per fifty square

Acoma pueblo.

miles—while east of the Mississippi lived an average of nine natives per fifty square miles.

Like human societies everywhere, these Indian cultures had
not been standing still. By 1492 North America had already seen
the rise and fall of an array of Native American civilizations.
From Canada to Florida, from the Atlantic Coast west to
Kansas, archaeologists have discovered over two million pre-
Columbian earth mounds, the result of the work of tens of
thousands of Native Americans. Some of the mounds were foundations of temples built by Ohio and Mississippi River valley
peoples. Collectively known as "Mound Builders," these Indian
nations had also produced striking art in pottery, copper, and
shell. Other mounds were burial sites, constructed by farming
groups who flourished over three thousand years ago. Excava-
tions at Cahokia, Illinois, near present-day East St. Louis, have
uncovered the remains of a prehistoric city, which once contained, it is estimated, from forty to sixty thousand inhabitants.
And throughout the canyons and mesas of southern Colorado
and northern New Mexico, pre-Columbian apartment houses can
still be visited, stone-and-adobe terraced dwellings skillfully
built up to four and five stories in height. Erected by the fabled
Anasazi, "the ancient ones," centuries before the arrival of the
white man, they were the homes of highly religious, democratic,
and peaceful farmers.

Some of these societies had disappeared entirely by the end
of the fifteenth century. Others were undergoing profound
social transformation. It is intriguing to imagine what civilizations might have developed if the natural evolutionary process
had been allowed to continue. Nonetheless, the white explorers
and settlers who brought it to a halt found an impressive range of
Indian groups. The word "tribe" does not do justice to the
extreme variety of their political organizations, methods of

food-gathering, cultural and religious patterns, and population size.

In the Northeast the first whites arrived after the five Iroquoian tribes had established a permanent political union. Their Great League, founded in the late fifteenth century by the legendary Hiawatha and Deganawida, was said to have been a model for the Founding Fathers when they designed the American republic. The combined might of the Iroquoian nations was so formidable that the French and British would be forced to negotiate with them as an equal sovereignty. In the Southeast, whites would encounter the thousands of loosely-knit Muskogean-speaking Indians who came to be known as the Creek Confederacy. In Louisiana they would encounter the last remnants of the aristocratic Natchez, whose caste society was ruled by an absolute monarch known as "The Sun." In Virginia they would discover that the Powhatan Confederacy linked together two hundred villages and thirty different tribes. In California they would stumble upon a seemingly endless succession of independent, isolated groups with widely different languages, bands so small they are better classified as tribelets.

These native bands, tribelets, pueblo city-states, nations, and confederacies were as culturally different from each other as the nations of Europe. Most had developed elaborate mythologies with explanations for the origin of every river, mountain, and valley in their region. In both the East and the West their territories were covered with "traces," networks of narrow, moccasin-worn paths, trails that had been followed by hunters and warriors for generations. In the Midwest and on the Great Plains their lands were crisscrossed with wider, equally ancient thoroughfares along which entire tribes intercepted migrating buffalo and cut through mountain ranges.

Thus North America was well discovered by the time

Columbus and his party set foot on its shores. But actually Columbus was not the first European to arrive. In fact, some scholars suggest that the first non-Indians came from Asia. There are Buddhist texts that tell of five beggar priests who sailed from China in A.D. 458. Drifting on the Japanese Current, they are believed to have landed either in Mexico or in Guatemala, a realm they called the Kingdom of Fu-Sang. And it has definitely been established that somewhere between A.D. 1006 and 1347, Viking seafarers from Scandinavia fought and traded with the natives of Greenland, Labrador, and Nova Scotia.

Curiously, in every corner of North America one can find tribal legends anticipating the white man's coming. On what is today Martha's Vineyard, an Indian seer said a great white whale would foretell the coming of a strange white race who would crowd out the red men. In Mexico there existed the myth of the bearded white god, Quetzalcoatl, who would return to reclaim his kingdom. Indeed, only a few years before 1519, when the first of the Spanish conquistadores, Hernando Cortez, arrived in Mexico, the Aztec emperor Montezuma saw ghostly people in his polished, volcanic-glass mirror: they seemed to be "coming massed, coming as conquerors, coming in war panoply. Deer bore them on their backs."

It is possible that some tribes received advance word of early Indian-white meetings, then turned these rumors into predictions. When you read the examples that follow of such prophecies, it is important to remember that "first contact," as the initial encounters between Native Americans and whites are termed by anthropologists, occurred at different times in different places. Generally, the more eastern and southern the locale, the earlier was the first contact. Thus the Hopi Indians of Arizona and the Hurons of eastern Canada had both experienced their first meeting with Europeans by about 1540. But the Sioux of the

Dakota plains would not have firsthand knowledge of them for another one hundred and fifty years; and the Wintun of northern California for a further half century.

Indian society was on the eve of what was to be the most catastrophic confrontation in its history. The Wasco Indians of Oregon have a prophecy story in which a wise old man dreams of strangers with hair on their faces coming from the direction of the rising sun. When he awakens, he gives this advice to his fellow tribesmen: "You people must be careful."

· 1 ·

He Will Use Any Means to Get What He Wants

Dan Katchongva—his Hopi surname means White Cloud Above Horizon—was a revered spiritual leader from Hotevilla, the most traditional of the Southwest's eleven Hopi towns. When he repeated this ancient prophecy in 1955, during testimony at a Washington congressional hearing, he was in his eighties. Within the oral tradition of the "peaceful ones," as the Hopi call themselves, are a number of legends foretelling the future of mankind. One of them mentions the Bahana, the Hopi's lost white brother, who vowed to return to the Hopi to establish peace and spread wisdom. The Hopi say they wait for him still.

In ancient times it was prophesied by our forefathers that this land would be occupied by the Indian people and then from somewhere a White Man would come. He will come either with a strong faith and righteous religion which the Great Spirit has also given to him, or he will come after he has abandoned that great Life Plan and fallen to a faith of his own personal ideas which he invented before coming here. It was known that the White Man is an intelligent person, an inventor of many words, a man who knows how to influence people because of his sweet way of talking and that he will use many of these things upon us when he comes. We knew that this land beneath us was composed of many things that we might want to use later such as mineral resources. We knew that this is the wealthiest part of this continent, because it is here the Great Spirit lives. We knew that the White Man will search for the things that look good to him, that he will use many good ideas in order to obtain his heart's desire, and we knew that if he had strayed from the Great Spirit he would use *any* means to get what he wants. These things we were warned to watch, and we today know that those prophecies were true because we can see how many new and selfish ideas and plans are being put before us. We know that if we accept these things we will lose our land and give up our very lives.

DAN KATCHONGVA, *Hopi*

· 2 ·

White Rabbit Got Lotsa Everything

In 1939, Lucy Young, a member of the Wintun tribe of northern California, told a local historian her life story. Although she was nearly blind from cataracts and over ninety years old at the time, her story-telling gifts remained sharp. The humorous, poignant events she recalls here probably took place in the 1840's, just before gold was discovered in Humboldt and Mendocino counties. Later in her reminiscences Mrs. Young describes her family's terrible experiences during the Gold Rush itself. The gold-rushers and homesteaders who flooded into California then were responsible for murdering over fifty thousand Native Americans between 1848 and 1870 alone.

My grandpa, before white people came, had a dream. He was so old he was all doubled up. Knees to chin, and eyes like indigo. Grown son carry him in great basket on his back, every place.

My grandpa say: "White Rabbit"—he mean white people—"gonta devour our grass, our seed, our living. We won't have nothing more, this world. Big elk with straight horn come when white man bring it." I think he meant cattle. " 'Nother animal, bigger than deer, but round feet, got hair on his neck." This one, horse, I guess.

My aunt say: "Oh, Father, you out your head, don't say that way."

He say: "Now, Daughter, I not crazy. You young people gonta see this."

People come long way, listen to him dream. He dream, then say this way, every morning.

They leave li'l children play by him. He watch good. Have big stick, wave round, scare snake away. He had good teeth. All old people had good teeth.

One time they travel, they come to big pile of brush. My grandpa stop, and look at it. He say: "This, good wood. When I die, burn my body to ashes on top of ground. Here gonta be big canoe, run around, carry white people's things. Those White Rabbit got lotsa everything."

Lucy Young.

"How canoe gonta run round on dry ground all round here?" we askum. "Don't know," he say. "Just run that way." He mean wagon, I guess.

I never grow much. They call me "Li'l Shorty," but I know pretty near everything that time. My grandpa put his head on my head, smoove my hair, and hold his hand there.

"Long time you gonta live, my child," he say. "You live long time in this world."

Well, I live long enough. I guess 'bout ninety-five next summer, if I living till then.

My grandpa never live to see white people, just dreaming every night 'bout them. People come long way, listen [to] him dream.

My grandpa move down by big spring. One day he couldn't get up. He say: "I gonta leave you today. I used to be good hunter, kill bear, elk, deer, feed my children. Can't feed my children no more. Like old root, just ready for growing now. Pretty soon dead. Speak no more."

All seem like dream to me. Long, long ago. Night-time, he die, and in morning, all tied up in deerskin with grass rope. Sit up knees to chin. They tie him up too soon. He roll over, and come back. Scare everybody. He ask for water, and ask for packstrap to basket always carry him in. He ask for li'l basket he always use for cup. He drink lots.

"I starve for water, and want my strap," he say. "That's why I come back."

Then he die. Our people dig big hole, put stick across. Put brush. Put body in. Put more brush. Burn all to ashes. They put basket and strap, too, with him, when he go where people go at last.

LUCY YOUNG, *Wintun*

· 3 ·
Visitors from Heaven

The artist Norval Morriseau painted a colorful mural that covered an entire wall of the Indians of Canada pavilion at Montreal's 1967 Exposition. But Morriseau, or Copper Thunderbird as he is known in his native Ojibway language, is a writer as well as a painter. In his book, Legends of My People, the Great Ojibway, *he narrates his grandfather's story of the conjuring of mysterious fabrics that presaged the white man's coming.*

The "shaking tent" performance he describes here was unique to the ceremonialism of the Great Lakes peoples. Inside the enclosure's skin or bark covering, the medicine man communicated with spirits who entered and left through a single opening at the top; those gathered outside witnessed the spirits shaking the tent and heard their eerie voices.

The Hudson's Bay Company mentioned in the selection was originally chartered in 1670 by English traders who were anxious to gain control of the traffic in beaver pelts. The company grew to dominate commerce in frontier Canada.

This story was told to my grandfather many years ago.

One time, about two hundred years ago, in a place called Fort Hope, Ontario, there was a settlement of Ojibway Indians where there was a medicine man who brought visitors from heaven to a huge wigwam shaped like a beaver house. Each spring the medicine man would make this great wigwam and place holes in the top and sides, so that the great wind, if it blew on the top, would also blow out the sides.

After everyone was seated in a big circle about ten feet from

The framework of an Ojibway "shaking tent."   (SMITHSONIAN INSTITUTION)

the tent, the medicine man inside would speak to the people outside and would say, "Now we shall have visitors again," and begin to pound his medicine drum. The great skies were clear, and there was no wind.

All of a sudden a wind was heard to blow from the heavens and into the top of the wigwam, and from the holes on the sides came a refreshing breeze. In mid-air a rustle of people was heard, but none were seen. Everyone was now looking and listening, and from inside the wigwam people, men and women, were heard talking. The medicine man inside spoke to the Indians without, saying, "Our visitors are here. Listen."

In those days the Indian people had never seen silk or satin, for everyone wore buckskin clothing. From the side of the opening on the wigwam appeared the finest silk in colors of red and blue and white. These, the Ojibway Indians believe, were the dresses of the visitors. The material came from the sides of the wigwam because the wind was blowing from heaven into the open top, forcing some of the clothing worn by the visitors to appear on the sides. After about an hour the drum was beaten again and the visitors were heard to leave. Everyone looked at the top, but nothing was to be seen and everything became quiet. Then the medicine man appeared at the door of the wigwam and spoke to his people, "My people, you have again seen and heard our visitors from heaven. Next spring we shall invite them again."

The old lady who told this to my grandfather about fifty years ago was very old; she was ninety-nine. She said, "We were all surprised, not at the great magic but at the material we saw at that time. For everyone then wore buckskin clothing and no silk or satin was known to the Indians. Afterwards, when the Hudson's Bay Company came to us, they brought with them the material we had previously seen and touched, that had blown out of the great medicine lodge."

NORVAL MORRISEAU, *Ojibway*

· 4 ·

Thunder's Dream Comes True

The Sauk Indian leader Black Hawk gained renown for the short-lived resistance he led in 1832 against federal troops; he was fighting to regain his Illinois homeland, which had been taken over by white settlers. Black Hawk was born in 1767 at the mouth of the Rock River. His precocious exploits as a young warrior against the Osage and the Cherokee, his intelligence, spellbinding oratory, and talent for summoning other tribes to his cause, place him among the foremost of Native America's "patriot chiefs." In his book, Black Hawk: An Autobiography, *first published in 1833, he recounts his great-grandfather's dream of the coming of the whites. The unnamed French visitor mentioned in the selection could have been Samuel de Champlain, who in 1611 established a trading post at Montreal.*

My great-grandfather, Nanàmakee, or Thunder (according to the tradition given me by my father, Pyesa), was born in the vicinity of Montreal, where the Great Spirit first placed the Sauk Nation, and inspired him with a belief that, at the end of four years, he should see a *white man*, who would be to him a father. Consequently he blacked his face, and ate but once a day (just as the sun was going down) for three years, and continued dreaming throughout all this time whenever he slept—when the Great Spirit again appeared to him, and told him, that, at the end of one year more, he should meet his father—and directed him to start seven days before its expiration and take with him his two brothers *Namah*, or Sturgeon, and *Paukahummawa*, or Sun Fish, and travel in a direction to the left of sun-rising. After pursuing this course five days, he sent out his two brothers to listen if they could hear a noise, and if so, to fasten some grass to the end of a pole, erect it, pointing in the direction of the sound, and then return to him.

Early next morning they returned, and reported that they had heard sounds which appeared near at hand, and that they had fulfilled his order. They all then started for the place where the pole had been erected; when, on reaching it, Nanàmakee left his party, and went alone to the place from whence the sounds proceeded, and found that the white man had arrived and pitched his tent. When he [Nanàmakee] came in sight, his father came out to meet him. He [the white man] took him by the hand, and welcomed him into his tent. He told him that he [the white man] was the son of the King of France—that he had been dreaming for four years—that the Great Spirit had directed him to come here, where he should meet a nation of people who had never yet seen a white man—that they should be his children, and he should be their father.

BLACK HAWK, *Sauk*

· 5 ·

Easy Life of the Gray-Eyed

The ancient Acoma Pueblo in New Mexico's Valencia County lies atop a steep rocky mesa 357 feet high. Today most of the "People of the White Rock" inhabit a newer village closer to the Rio Grande River—sixty miles from Acoma. But in summertime many families return to their adobe houses high on the mesa. Then the narrow, dusty streets bustle as in the old days. James Paytiamo spent his childhood there, and his reminiscence of daily life at Acoma, Flaming Arrow's People, *was published in 1932. This excerpt differs from the other prophecy stories in that during Paytiamo's childhood, the existence of the white man was an established fact. What the wise old Acoma caciques, or headmen, here foretell is the destructive influences white culture will have on the traditional Acoma way of life.*

I can just remember the old men of my village. Old age was simply a delightful time, when the old men sat on the sunny door-steps, playing in the sun with the children, until they fell asleep. At last they failed to wake up.

These old, old men used to prophesy about the coming of the white man. They would go about tapping with their canes on the adobe floor of the house, and call to us children:

"Listen! Listen! The gray-eyed people are coming nearer and nearer. They are building an iron road. They are coming nearer every day. There will be a time when you will mix with these people. That is when the Gray Eyes are going to get you to drink black, hot water, which you will drink whenever you eat. Then your teeth will become soft. They will get you to smoke at a young age, so that your eyes will run tears on windy days, and your eyesight will be poor. Your joints will crack when you want to move slowly and softly.

"You will sleep on soft beds and will not like to rise early. When you begin to wear heavy clothes and sleep under heavy covers, then you will grow lazy. Then there will be no more singing heard in the valleys as you walk.

"When you begin to eat with iron sticks, your tones will grow louder. You will speak louder and overtalk your parents. You will grow disobedient. Then when you mix with these gray-eyed people, you will learn their ways, you will break up homes, and murder and steal."

Such things have come true, and I compare my generation with the old generation. We are not good as they were; neither are we healthy as they were.

How did these old men know what was coming? That is what I would like to know.

JAMES PAYTIAMO, *Acoma Pueblo*

· 6 ·
The Spider's Web

One of the classics of Native American literature is Black Elk
Speaks, *the autobiography of an Oglala Sioux holy man, recorded
by John G. Neihardt, a noted Nebraskan poet. By the end of the
nineteenth century, Black Elk, a relative of the famous Sioux
leader Crazy Horse, had seen his tribe transformed from buffalo-
hunting lords of the Great Plains to hungry, impoverished
prisoners, pent up on thirteen government reservations. At the
age of nine, Black Elk had gone into a trance and experienced a
wondrous vision in which the Six Grandfathers—West, East,
North, South, Earth, and Sky—granted him unusual spiritual
powers. Thereafter he was dedicated "to bringing to life the
flowering tree of his people" by revitalizing the seven sacred rites
of the Oglala. In this brief selection Black Elk remembers the
ominous dream of an earlier Sioux medicine man.*

A long time ago my father told me what his father told him,
that there was once a Lakota [Sioux] holy man, called Drinks
Water, who dreamed what was to be; and this was long before
the coming of the Wasichus [white men]. He dreamed that the
four-leggeds were going back into the earth and that a strange
race had woven a spider's web all around the Lakotas. And he
said: "When this happens, you shall live in square gray houses,
in a barren land, and beside those square gray houses you shall
starve."

They say he went back to Mother Earth soon after he saw
this vision, and it was sorrow that killed him. You can look about

A rare early picture of Black Elk (left), *taken when he was on an extended European dance tour*.   (smithsonian institution)

you now and see that he meant these dirt-roofed houses we are living in, and that all the rest was true. Sometimes dreams are wiser than waking.

black elk, *Oglala Sioux*

FACE TO FACE

I n 1006 a Viking ship, captained by Thorvald, son of Eric the Red, landed somewhere along the coast of Nova Scotia. We will never know what the *Skrellings*—"barbarians" or "weaklings," as the Vikings termed the natives—felt when the two peoples first set eyes on each other. They cannot have remained neutral for long, however. Minutes after landing, Thorvald's sailors killed eight of them.

On Friday, October 12, 1492, when Christopher Columbus and his men hauled their armed landing boat up on the island in the Bahamas to which he gave the name San Salvador, the local Taino Indians were awestruck. "They believe very firmly that I, with these ships and crew, came from the sky," Columbus wrote in his journal, "and in such opinion they received me at every place where I landed, after they lost their terror." We do not know if the Taino were less respectful after Columbus forcibly took ten of them to Spain to display at the court of King Ferdinand and Queen Isabella. Two years later he shipped off five hundred West Indian natives as slaves; nearly all of them died of disease. Thus began the wholesale enslavement of

The Cheyennes' first encounter with white men, on the Missouri River, as portrayed by the nineteenth-century Cheyenne artist, Howling Wolf.

(JOSLYN ART MUSEUM, OMAHA, NEBRASKA)

the Indians by Spain, which virtually annihilated the native peoples of the Caribbean.

The explorers, treasure hunters, traders, missionaries, trappers, soldiers, and colonists who followed in the wake of Columbus represented a number of separate cultures. Each brought to the New World their own national characteristics and particular interests.

Spain viewed the Indians both as potential converts to Catholicism and as slave labor for its silver mines in Mexico and the Southwest and its plantations in the Caribbean. The battle-hardened gold-and-glory-seeking conquistadors left small outposts in their wake—the missions and scattered land-grant colonies. But Spain never settled there on a massive scale. Following the explorations of Hernando de Soto (1539–42) and Francisco Coronado (1540–42), St. Augustine was founded (1565) to secure Spain's claim to the Florida peninsula, and Santa Fe would later (1609) become the capital of the Southwest. But the region known as New Spain—extending unbrokenly down the Pacific Coast from Vancouver Island to the tip of South America and inland as far east as the Mississippi River, with the Florida peninsula as an isolated holding—was held mainly in the futile hope that it would add to the wealth and power of Spain.

France was always associated with tribes and territories which could be visited via inland waterways. Their first New World explorer, Jacques Cartier, saw the St. Lawrence River in 1534 and was warmly welcomed by five local Huron Indians there a year later. Of all the newcomers, the French were probably the most congenial to the Indians. While the Spanish sanctioned white-Indian marriages after the fact, they fundamentally considered the Native Americans to be both pagan and inferior. The French, on the other hand, often became absorbed in Indian life, adopting Indian customs and dress, learning native languages, and intermarrying. As the French voyageurs paddled their canoes up and down the rivers of the New World, their main goal was to dominate the fur trade. French exploration reached its height with Robert de La Salle's arrival at the Gulf of Mexico in 1682. Within the expanse that was claimed as New France—west of the Appalachian Mountains to the Mississippi River, south from Canada to the Gulf of Mexico—the French established a few major towns like Quebec (1608) and Montreal (1642). But they were generally busier forging their trade network than building a permanent empire.

The English colonists were a different breed altogether. The families who began populating the South after Jamestown's founding (1607) and the religious idealists and middle-class townsfolk who founded the more northern settlements, such as Plymouth, Massachusetts (1620), had come to stay, to transplant their own civilization in the New World. The Puritans and Pilgrims even hoped to improve that civilization with stricter religious discipline. Unlike England's governmental representatives—the soldiers and traders—these dissident colonists had little use for Indians. The Indians were "savages" (being hunters) and "devil-worshipers" (not being Christians); they were nuisances who blocked the growth of civilization in this new English-speaking colonial world.

Just as the white man discovered many different Indian ways of life, so the Indian learned that the white man came with many different languages and national personalities. Besides the Spanish, French, and English, there were explorers and traders from Portugal, Sweden, Denmark, Holland, and even Russia. Then, too, Frenchmen in Canada behaved differently from Frenchmen in Louisiana. English-speaking people presented at least three regional personalities—in the North, the South, and along the

Cumberland Mountains. When the three major European nations—England, France, and Spain—began their struggle for domination of the New World, each looked for Indian allies to fight alongside them. The tribes made compacts, declared war, or remained neutral, based on their first impressions of these varied brands of white men.

The last "first contact" occurred in 1818 when the polar Eskimos, encountering a British naval expedition, learned they were not the only humans on earth. By then, virtually every other Indian tribe in North America had already made some sort of accommodation to the white presence.

Some early Indian/white encounters had boded well. Others immediately erupted into hostility, usually because the Indians had been forewarned about the aggressive intentions of the foreigners. Such was the case with the Zuñi Indians of the Rio Grande. In the summer of 1540, they sent their women and children into hiding just prior to the arrival of the conquistador they had never seen, Francisco Coronado. He promptly killed twelve of the Zuñi warriors protecting their leading town of Hawikuh, then sacked it. Other tribes shared the instinctive reaction of the proud Kiowa of the Plains, who could not tolerate the presence of "ears sticking out" and "growlers"—two Kiowa names for whites—in their hunting grounds.

Stories based on these dramatic face-to-face encounters became a part of tribal folklore. It is interesting how many of the selections that follow underscore the cultural conflicts that have plagued Indian/white relations down to the present day.

· 1 ·

Their Wondrous Works
and Ways

*In 1862 the eastern Sioux Indians, the Santee of Minnesota, rose
up against white settlers, killing over 450 men, women, and children within a week. American retaliation was swift, and Charles
Alexander Eastman, then four years old, was among the Santee
refugees who fled to Canada for sanctuary. When his father
was turned over to United States authorities, relatives raised
the boy near Fort Ellis in southern Manitoba.*

*Born with the Indian name, "the Pitiful Last," but later called
"the Winner" (Ohiyesa), Eastman did not see a white person until he was sixteen. He then became one of a stream of Indians who
since the eighteenth century had attended Dartmouth College. In 1890 he earned his medical degree from Boston University. Just after the turn of the century his books on Sioux life
and philosophy gained great popularity, especially among young
readers. In this selection from the autobiographical work,
Indian Boyhood (1902), Eastman recalls his own amazement
at his uncle's eyewitness report on white culture.*

I had heard marvelous things of this people. In some things we
despised them; in others we regarded them as *wakan* (mysterious), a race whose power bordered upon the supernatural. I
learned that they had made a "fireboat." I could not understand
how they could unite two elements which cannot exist together.
I thought the water would put out the fire, and the fire would
consume the boat if it had the shadow of a chance. This was to

Charles Alexander Eastman.

me a preposterous thing! But when I was told that the Big Knives had created a "fire-boat-walks-on-mountains" (a locomotive) it was too much to believe. . . .

I had seen guns and various other things brought to us by the French Canadians, so that I had already some notion of the supernatural gifts of the white man; but I had never before heard such tales as I listened to that morning. It was said that they had bridged the Missouri and Mississippi rivers, and that they made immense houses of stone and brick, piled on top of one another until they were as high as high hills. My brain was puzzled with these things for many a day. Finally I asked my uncle why the Great Mystery gave such power to the *Washichu* (the rich)—sometimes we called them by this name—and not to us Dakotas [Sioux].

"For the same reason," he answered, "that he gave to Duta the skill to make fine bows and arrows, and to Wachesne no skill to make anything."

"And why do the Big Knives increase so much more in numbers than the Dakotas?" I continued.

"It has been said, and I think it must be true, that they have larger families than we do. I went into the house of an *Eashicha* (a German), and I counted no less than nine children. The eldest of them could not have been over fifteen. When my grandfather first visited them, down at the mouth of the Mississippi, they were comparatively few; later my father visited their Great Father at Washington, and they had already spread over the whole country.

"Certainly they are a heartless nation. They have made some of their people servants—yes, slaves! We have never believed in keeping slaves, but it seems that these *Washichu* do! It is our belief that they painted their servants black a long time ago, to tell them from the rest, and now the slaves have children born to them of the same color!

"The greatest object of their lives seems to be to acquire possessions—to be rich. They desire to possess the whole world. For thirty years they were trying to entice us to sell them our land. Finally the outbreak [Minnesota, 1862] gave them all, and we have been driven away from our beautiful country.

"They are a wonderful people. They have divided the day into hours, like the moons of the year. In fact, they measure everything. Not one of them would let so much as a turnip go from his field unless he received full value for it. I understand that their great men make a feast and invite many, but when the feast is over the guests are required to pay for what they have eaten before leaving the house. I myself saw at White Cliff (the name given to St. Paul, Minnesota) a man who kept a brass drum and a bell to call people to his table; but when he got them in he would make them pay for the food!

"I am also informed," said my uncle, "but this I hardly believe, that their Great Chief (President) compels every man to pay him for the land he lives upon and all his personal goods—even for his own existence—every year!" (This was his idea of taxation.) "I am sure we could not live under such a law. . . .

"In war they have leaders and war-chiefs of different grades. The common warriors are driven forward like a herd of antelopes to face the foe. It is on account of this manner of fighting—from compulsion and not from personal bravery—that we count no *coup* on them. A lone warrior can do much harm to a large army of them in a bad country."

It was this talk with my uncle that gave me my first clear idea of the white man.

CHARLES ALEXANDER EASTMAN, *Santee Sioux*

· 2 ·

Before They Got Thick

This tale of the Lipan Apache reads like a southwestern version of the story of the Plymouth Colony: Native Americans help white pioneers survive by bringing them gifts of pumpkin seed and seed corn and showing them how to plant them. Related by Percy Bigmouth in 1935, it describes events that probably took place in the early nineteenth century when his ancestors were living near the Texas-Louisiana border. During the Indian wars in the Southwest (1845–56), when official policy in Texas called for the brutal extermination of all Indians, the Lipan hid in Mexico. Eventually they made their home with their kinsmen, the Mescalero Apache, in New Mexico.

My grandmother used to tell this story; she told it to my mother. It is about the time when they lived near the gulf. She says that they lived at a place called "Beside the Smooth Water." They used to camp there on the sand. Sometimes a big wave would come up and then they would pick up many seashells. Sometimes they used to find water turtles. They used to find fish too and gather them and eat them.

One time they had a big wave. It was very bad. They thought the ocean was going to come right up. It came up a long way. Living things from the water covered the bank, were washed up. Then, when the sun came out and it was hot all these things began to swell and smelled bad.

One day they looked over the big water. Then someone saw a little black dot over on the water. He came back and told that he had seen that strange thing. Others came out. They sat there and looked. It was getting larger. They waited. Pretty soon it came up. It was a boat. The boat came to the shore. The Indians went back to the big camp. All the Indians came over and watched. People were coming out. They looked at those people coming out. They saw that the people had blue eyes and were white. They thought these people might live in the water all the time.

They held a council that night. They were undecided whether they should let them live or kill them.

One leader said, "Well, they have a shape just like ours. The difference is that they have light skin and hair."

Another said, "Let's not kill them. They may be a help to us some day. Let's let them go and see what they'll do."

So the next day they watched them. "What shall we call them?" they asked. . . .

Some still wanted to kill them. Others said no. So they decided to let them alone.

The Lipan went away. After a year they said, "Let's go back and see them."

They did so. Only a few were left. Many had starved to death. Some said, "Let's kill them now; they are only a few." But others said, "No, let us be like brothers to them."

It was spring. The Lipan gave them some pumpkin seed and seed corn and told them how to use it. The people took it and after that they got along all right. They raised a little corn and some pumpkins. They started a new life. Later on the Lipan left for a while. When they returned, the white people were getting along very well. The Lipan gave them venison. They were getting along very well. After that, they began to get thick.

PERCY BIGMOUTH, *Lipan Apache*

· 3 ·

Silmoodawa Gives a Complete Performance

Following the example set by Christopher Columbus, the Spanish conquistador Hernando Cortez continued the ritual of sending Indians to Europe in order to parade them before royalty.

At the court of Charles V, Aztecs posed for artists and juggled for gawking lords and ladies. Later, in the eighteenth century, Indian chiefs went abroad to discuss disputed territorial boundaries and present petitions. And in 1827, a party of Osage Indians undertook a three-year sightseeing tour of France. Such trips were encouraged not only for the entertainment Indians provided, but because officials wished to impress Native Americans with the splendors of Europe and the power of their governments. In 1870 an anonymous Micmac Indian—from Canada's Maritime Provinces—told the early Indian scholar the Reverend Silas T. Rand the following story about one "Real Live Indian" who turned the tables on his aristocratic audience.

Shortly after the country was discovered by the French, an Indian named Silmoodawa was taken to Planchean [France] as a curiosity. Among other curious adventures, he was prevailed upon to exhibit the Indian mode of killing and curing game. A fat ox or deer was brought out of a beautiful park and handed over to the Indian; he was provided with all the necessary implements, and placed within an enclosure of ropes, through which no person was allowed to pass, but around which multitudes were gathered to witness the butchering operations of the savage.

He shot the animal with a bow, bled him, skinned and dressed him, sliced up the meat, and spread it out on flakes to dry; he then cooked a portion and ate it, and in order to exhibit the whole process, and to take a mischievous revenge upon them for making an exhibition of him, he went into a corner of the yard and eased himself before them all.

ANONYMOUS, *Micmac*

· 4 ·

A Different Kind of Man

This melancholy tale of a solitary white man who spent years among the Assiniboine of the northern Great Plains was told by Bad Hawk to James Larpenteur Long (First Boy), a half-Assiniboine historian of his people. A trader's clerk, cattleman, grocery-store owner, tribal official, and a member of the men's secret warrior society, Long interviewed Bad Hawk in the 1930's as part of a government-sponsored oral-history program. The identity of Lone White Man is lost forever.

My granduncle, Tall Man, was a member of a war party of about twelve, that camped on the south side of the Missouri River, above where the government has built the great Fort Peck Dam.

When the party resumed their journey early the next morning, the two scouts, who had left earlier, came running back. "There is a strange man walking towards the river with a gun on his shoulder," they said. So the party circled about and hid in the path of the man.

When he came closer, one from the party rose and walked towards him, at the same time lifting his hand as a sign for the man to stop. In sign language he was asked as to what tribe he belonged, but instead of an answer the man dropped his gun and raised his hands high above his head.

The rest of the party, when they saw the act, ran over and surrounded the man. Several spoke up, "Don't any of you kill him, he is a different kind of man, let's look him over."

He stood there terrified and continued to look from one to the other.

Probably made to commemorate an early encounter with whites, this Chumash rock painting in Southern California's Santa Monica Mountains includes four non-Indians on horseback. (Call to California—A COPLEY BOOK)

The man was tall and his hair was down to his shoulders. With the exception of his forehead, eyes, and nose, his face was covered with a heavy beard. His chest, his arms down to the tops of his hands, and his legs were covered with a hairy growth. Nothing like that had ever been seen among the tribe, only animals were that way.

"This must be what is called a white man, that we have heard about," they said among themselves.

His clothing was torn to shreds, and he was thin and seemed to be starved. Apparently all he had had for food were several pieces of a large cactus that he had peeled. These he kept in the shot bag that was attached to the powder horn. They took him along, made camp right away, and prepared some food, which he devoured like a hungry animal.

He stayed with the war party until they returned home. Fortunately for the white man, there were no encounters with the enemy on that trip.

My granduncle took the man home and new clothing was made for him. The man gave the gun, which was without ammunition, to my granduncle. He stayed with our people for many years and my granduncle adopted him as a brother, because they were about the same age and height. He was named Lone White Man.

When he learned our language, he told of being with a party of white men who came up the Missouri River. He was with a group of hunters who supplied game for the party. When the crew started their journey upstream each day, the hunters traveled away from the river, then paralleled it until they joined the crew at the night camp with game killed that day.

On one of those jaunts, Lone White Man failed to meet the party. Each day he expected to find them, but after several days he came to the conclusion that he was lost. As he had enough ammunition to last only a day or so, it was not long before he was out [of game] entirely. Berries and roots were all he had to eat after that.

On the morning that he was seen by the war party, he was on his way to the river, thinking he might see a boat. He had kept near the river all the time hoping to find his party.

Even after the whites were numerous, Lone White Man showed no desire to leave our people. One day he met one of the steamboats and did some trading. Among other things, he brought home some bacon and a frying pan. He told my granduncle that he had wanted fried liver and bacon for so long that he was going to satisfy that desire. He prepared a large stack of fried liver and bacon on which he feasted all alone. With so many different kinds of meat to be had at that time, our people never ate liver, which they used only for tanning hides.

Lone White Man lived among our people for many years, but never married. Granduncle never told if the man died out here or finally left the country.

FIRST BOY, *Assiniboine*

· 5 ·

I Hid Myself and Watched

To have peered as a child at strangely dressed, hairy-faced, sunburned, edgy, loud-voiced strangers must have been a common "first-contact" experience for many Indians. In the first of the two selections that follow, Pretty Shield, a Crow woman from Montana, tells of an encounter with white trappers, men who were probably in the employ of a Missouri River fur company, which must have taken place about 1860. In the second, a Navajo from western New Mexico, known to us only as Jaime, remembers the day, a half century later, when bearded strangers surprised him in the midst of a Navajo boy's most common chore—sheepherding.

When I was six snows old . . . these white men, trappers, with many packhorses, came to our village. At first my people did not call the white man *Masta-cheeda* (yellow-eyes) as they do now. Our first name for the white man was *Beta-awk-a-wah-cha* (Sits on the Water) because my people first saw the white man in a canoe on Big river. The canoe was far off. The white man in it looked as though he sat on the water; and so my people named him, and his tribe. . . .

The three white trappers wore beards that did not look nice.

Pretty Shield.

And yet one of those men had kindly eyes, I remember. I saw a little girl shake hands with him. There was white in one's beard, I noticed. All the others' were brown. I hid myself and watched the three go into the lodge of our chief, Walks with the Moon. I did not see inside, nor hear what was said in the lodge of Walks with the Moon, and yet I know that the three white men gave the Chief some tobacco, and that they smoked with him, saying that they had traveled a long time looking for the Crows. My mother told me that these white men had asked if they might stay with our people, and that Walks with the Moon had answered "No," giving them a night and a day to rest before going away. When, the next morning, I looked to see the white man with the kindly eyes he was gone. I never saw him again.

Later, when I was eleven years old, three other men who wore beards, but who were not white men, came to our people. These three caused trouble. I do not remember what it was that they did to make my people angry; but I know that two of them were killed. The other one lived for a long time with our people.

PRETTY SHIELD, *Crow*

One day I saw a man coming along with big white whiskers all over his face. The skin that showed was around his eyes, just a little bit. I had never seen a white man before. I ran away home and told the people I had seen something out there coming toward the sheep. It looked like a man, I said, but had wool all over its face. I thought the whiskers were wool, and I wasn't sure it was a man.

Roberto, my grandfather, was sitting outside the hogan having coffee and Navajo bread. He said, "That must have been a white man you seen." Pretty soon the man came up, walked up to Roberto, reached under his vest, and pulled out below the left arm a bunch of chili peppers. He peeled off three and gave them to Roberto, then he pointed to the bread and then down his throat. The women didn't want to feed him, but Roberto said, "Give him some." The pile of bread soon went away down.

Then the white man stood up, pointed away to the west, and walked off that way. Next day some of the Indian boys trailed him to see which way he was going. They found where he had spent the night, dug a hole and lit a tiny fire and laid down by it all night. Then his tracks went on toward the west.

JAIME, *Navajo*

COPYRIGHT
Ernest Brown
(24845)

INSIDE FORT PITT
1885

EXCHANGE BETWEEN WORLDS

At the time of the Creation, the Cherokee say, the white man was given a stone, and the Indian a piece of silver. Despising the stone, the white man threw it away. Finding the silver equally worthless, the Indian discarded it. Later the white man pocketed the silver as a source of material power; the Indian revered the stone as a source of sacred power. This prophetic story underscores the profound differences in Indian and white value systems. In time the Indian would be forced to use the white man's currency as his medium of exchange, but the white man would never appreciate the Indian's sense of the cosmic power invested in an ordinary pebble.

Long before the coming of "the makers of hatchets," as whites were called by the Iroquois, Indians throughout the continent of North America had traded with each other. In the Far West a popular trading spot was the present-day Oregon town of The Dalles. Here a salmon-rich stretch of boiling rapids on the Columbia River divides the world of the Pacific Coast from that of the inland Plateau. To this hub of thriving Indian commerce,

Cree trappers bringing beaver skins to the Hudson's Bay post at Fort Pitt in Canada. (PROVINCIAL ARCHIVES OF ALBERTA)

controlled by Chinook Indian traders who even exacted tolls along the river, came goods from the Northwest, the Great Plains, the Great Basin, and sometimes from as far away as the Great Lakes. Dealings were conducted in a universal trading language, a potpourri of Salish, Nootka, and Chinook words.

In California the Pomo bartered their homemade strings of disk shell beads for abalone and dried kelp from the coastal Yuki, fiber cord and sinew-baked bows from the forest-dwelling Patwin, and furs and iris cord from the inland Yuki. Farther east, Native American trade was just as active. The agricultural Hurons routinely exchanged their corn to the northern Nipissing, a hunting people, for fish and venison. Copper from northern Michigan found its way to tribes in Virginia. Obsidian, red pipestone, colored slate, flint, and salt were transported over long distances, from village to village.

The first commercial exchange between Indians and whites probably took place in the eleventh century, when natives of Nova Scotia received Viking knives and axes in return for gray fox and sable pelts. In the years ahead, this swap—the exchange of furs for metal—was to become the core of Indian and white commerce.

In the fifteenth and sixteenth centuries, as timber, fur-bearing animals, and other natural resources became scarcer in the Old World, Europeans looked across the seas for raw materials. The majority of the renowned early explorers of North America—men like John and Sebastian Cabot (1497), Jacques Cartier (1534), and Henry Hudson (1609)—were actually business agents on the lookout for new markets. Before long, the French, the English, the Dutch—and later the Americans—were competing for exclusive trading privileges with Indian tribes, enticing them with bribes of trinkets, liquor, and guns.

Indians guided Europeans to salt, tobacco, wood, and fish

which they then managed to harvest and ship back across the Atlantic. But in collecting furs and hides, native expertise and manpower were essential. Indians possessed skills to lure and trap animals and techniques for skinning and soft-tanning hides. They then transported these semifinished goods to white trading posts or waterfront docks. As Indians were encouraged to abandon intertribal trade and devote themselves exclusively to cleaning out the hidden stream dens of mink, marten, ermine, otter, sable, and muskrat, it was the beaver which came to enjoy highest value. Europe's hatmakers were building a multimillion-dollar industry. Whether for their furs, in the North, or for tanned deerskins, the main native commodity in the South, Indians received a range of new goods they quickly found indispensable: knives, the popular tomahawk, scissors, awls, needles, woolen cloth, mirrors, hawk bells, German silver to pound into ornaments, sheet metal to file into arrowheads and lance heads, brass kettles, "demon rum" (from the English), brandy (from the French), and above all, muskets, powder, and shot. By the mid-seventeenth century, such items had become an integral part of woodland Indian life.

Preferring to do business via the rivers, the French fur traders stowed their goods in forty-foot-long birchbark cargo canoes. The English packed their stores on muleback and rode overland to bargain with Indians. Eventually, toward the end of the eighteenth century, individual peddler-traders would be largely replaced by companies that operated a string of frontier trading outposts. Indians hauled their prime winter pelts to these posts in the spring, or bartered with company agents who caught up with tribes on the move.

All this trade transformed patterns of Indian life that had existed unchanged for centuries. Suddenly tribes found themselves competing for white business. As trapping sites were stripped of beaver, Indians battled among themselves for more westerly, fur-rich lands. Commercial agreements between the French and Huron Indians, for example, so angered the Iroquois that they joined forces with both the Dutch and the British, getting ample supplies of firearms in return. This alliance not only contributed decisively to British victory in the French and Indian War, it also enabled the Iroquois to ruthlessly dominate the northeastern fur trade.

When the rebellious colonies—the "thirteen fires" as the Iroquois called them—won independence from England, the United States entered this commercial war. Some posts along the Missouri River profited, but northward the Canadian Blackfoot refused to do business with the Americans. They resented the American habit of sending out white trappers—the legendary mountain men who were indebted to Indians for learning to maneuver in the wilderness—to compete against them in their own territory.

By 1840 high silk hats had become the fashion, and the fur trade was drying up. The Rocky Mountain beaver was nearly extinct. For a while a market in buffalo hides filled the vacuum, but soon white hunters with .50 caliber rifles made those animals just as rare. Between 1872 and 1874 over three and a half million buffalo were slaughtered for their hides, the meat left to rot on the plains.

Thanks in large part to the Indian, North America's natural resources greatly enriched European and American lives and pocketbooks. But white goods had a far more profound effect on the Indian world. In the Northeast, for example, traditional intertribal commerce was shattered in large measure by the new intense focus on one commodity—furs. With the animals gone, the prosperity Indians had enjoyed as a result of trade with whites was followed for many by a penniless dependency on white goods, especially on the powder and shot they now needed to protect themselves and to hunt for food. Meanwhile many white traders had proved themselves unscrupulous, manipulating their Native American customers with watered-down liquor spiced with tobacco and red pepper and dealing in shoddy, mass-produced goods.

Farther west, on the Great Plains, Native American life had been transformed by the arrival of the horse. When Antonio de Espejo first rode into Hopi land in 1583, the Indians—who had never before seen a horse—paved the ground with ceremonial kilts for the sacred beasts to walk upon. By the end of the seventeenth century, Wyoming Shoshonis were getting horses from Colorado Utes who had stolen them from Spanish settlements in New Mexico. The eastern Sioux, a canoeing people in the 1760's, were a mounted people thirty years later. The rapid spread of the horse throughout the Plains caused the flowering of an entirely new Indian way of life characterized by the Apaloosa-riding, war-bonneted warrior who would represent American Indianism around the world.

For the crop-raising Pueblo Indians along the Rio Grande in the Southwest, metal hoes and shovels and European vegetables made life easier but had no deeper effect upon tribal customs. The Navajo way of life, however, was eventually transformed by Spanish sheep and goats. Originally a hunting people, the Navajo became expert shepherds, making their livelihood by trading animals they had bred and blankets from the wool they had woven. Along the Northwest Coast the traditional wood carvings grew brighter as artisans applied European housepaints to their cedar totem poles. On the Plains silk ribbons, pearl buttons, red and blue cloth, Venetian and English glass beads, were added to native costumes. But trade goods sometimes hastened the decline of ancient crafts, such as pottery and porcupine-quill embroidery.

The western trading posts gave migratory groups a new focal

point for their wanderings, as well as expanded contact with neighboring tribes. In the spring Indians who might otherwise be blood enemies would pitch camp side by side, and bargain away their stocks of prime winter pelts. Later it was often at these same stockaded trading posts that defeated Indian leaders met governmental representatives of the United States to discuss terms of surrender and treaties of peace. By then the Indians' principal source of wealth—furs and hides—had been exhausted. All they had left that interested the white man was their land, which could usually be acquired without fair exchange.

The selections that follow offer glimpses of various Native American responses to white goods and frontier commerce.

· 1 ·

Thunder, Dizzying Liquid, and Cups That Do Not Grow

The white man's magical offerings—guns and metal utensils and liquor—all play a part in this Menomini folktale. The time is around the 1660's; the "sea" in the story is probably Lake Michigan; the Frenchmen are very likely traders who followed in the wake of the French missionary-explorer Jean Nicolet; the speaker is named Waioskasit.

As their trade with the French blossomed, the Menomini exchanged their sedentary life, contentedly cultivating wild rice, for a seminomadic existence as fur trappers. This bound them more tightly to the French, who encouraged them to buy goods on credit against future payment in furs. Yet the partnership, strengthened by extensive intermarriage, also made the Menomini a dominant power in the Great Lakes area.

When the Menomini lived on the shore of the sea, they one day were looking out across the water and observed some large vessels, which were near to them and wonderful to behold. Suddenly there was a terrific explosion, as of thunder, which startled the people greatly.

When the vessels approached the shore, men with light-colored skin landed. Most of them had hair on their faces, and they carried on their shoulders heavy sticks ornamented with shining metal. As the strangers came toward the Indians, the latter believed the leader to be a great manido [spirit], with his companions.

It is customary, when offering tobacco to a manido, to throw it into the fire, that the fumes may ascend to him and that he may be inclined to grant their request; but as this light-skin manido came in person, the chief took some tobacco and rubbed it on his forehead. The strangers appeared desirious of making friends with the Indians, and all sat on the ground and smoked. Then some of the strangers brought from the vessel some parcels which contained a liquid, of which they drank, finally offering some to the Menomini. The Indians, however, were afraid to drink such a pungent liquor indiscriminately, fearing it would kill them; therefore four useless old men were selected to drink the liquor, and thus to be experimented on, that it might be found whether the liquid would kill them or not.

The men drank the liquid, and although they had previously been very silent and gloomy, they now began to talk and to grow amused. Their speech flowed more and more freely, while the remainder of the Indians said, "See, now it is beginning to take effect!" Presently the four old men arose, and while walking about seemed very dizzy, when the Indians said, "See, now they are surely dying!" Presently the men dropped down and became unconscious; then the Indians said to one another, "Now they are dead; see what we escaped by not drinking the liquid!" There were sullen looks directed toward the strangers, and murmurings of destroying them for the supposed treachery were heard.

Before things came to a dangerous pass, however, the four old men got up, rubbed their eyes, and approached their kindred, saying, "The liquor is good, and we have felt very happy; you must try it, too." Notwithstanding the rest of the tribe were afraid to drink it then, they recalled the strangers, who were about to return to their boats.

The chief of the strangers next gave the Indians some flour, but they did not know what to do with it. The white chief then showed the Indians some biscuits, and told them how they were baked. When that was over, one of the white men presented to an Indian a gun, after firing it to show how far away anything could be killed. The Indian was afraid to shoot it, fearing the gun would knock him over, but the stranger showed the Indian how to hold it and to point it at a mark; then pulling the trigger, it made a terrific noise, but did not harm the Indian at all, as he had expected. Some of the Indians then accepted guns from the white strangers.

Next the white chief brought out some kettles and showed the Indians how to boil water in them. But the kettles were too large and too heavy to carry about, so the Indians asked that they be given small ones—cups as large as a clenched fist, for they believed they would grow to be large ones by and by.

The Indians received some small cups, as they desired, when the strangers took their departure. But the cups never grew to be kettles.

WAIOSKASIT, *Menomini*

· 2 ·
Keep Your Presents

A Pawnee, Curly Chief, recollects here a fellow tribesman's re-
jection of European wares. Actually a federation of four central
Plains peoples, the Pawnee lived in earth-lodge villages along
the Platte River in Nebraska. In the early decades of the nine-
teenth century, their lands lay in the path of American pioneers
whose wagons were rolling toward the Southwest. This contact
with whites brought them social dissolution and disease—in
1849 they lost a fourth of their people to smallpox and cholera.
In 1875 the tribe was moved to northern Oklahoma. There is no
record of which treaty session Curly Chief is remembering here.

I heard that long ago there was a time when there were no people in this country except Indians. After that, the people began
to hear of men that had white skins; they had been seen far to
the east. Before I was born, they came out to our country and
visited us. The man who came was from the Government. He
wanted to make a treaty with us, and to give us presents, blankets
and guns, and flint and steel, and knives.

The Head Chief told him that we needed none of these things.
He said, "We have our buffalo and our corn. These things the
Ruler gave to us, and they are all that we need. See this robe.
This keeps me warm in winter. I need no blanket."

The white men had with them some cattle, and the Pawnee
Chief said, "Lead out a heifer here on the prairie." They led her
out, and the Chief, stepping up to her, shot her through behind

the shoulder with his arrow, and she fell down and died. Then the Chief said, "Will not my arrow kill? I do not need your guns." Then he took his stone knife and skinned the heifer, and cut off a piece of fat meat. When he had done this, he said, "Why should I take your knives? The Ruler has given me something to cut with."

Then taking the fire sticks, he kindled a fire to roast the meat, and while it was cooking, he spoke again and said, "You see, my

Curly Chief (front row, third from left), *in a portrait by the noted western photographer, William Henry Jackson.* (PHILLIP MATTHEWS)

brother, that the Ruler has given us all that we need; the buffalo for food and clothing; the corn to eat with our dried meat; bows, arrows, knives and hoes; all the implements which we need for killing meat, or for cultivating the ground. Now go back to the country from whence you came. We do not want your presents, and we do not want you to come into our country."

CURLY CHIEF, *Pawnee*

· 3 ·

Give Us Good Goods

Trade often led to a dependency on white goods. Indians could not turn away from such conveniences as brass kettles and cloth once they became accustomed to them, or such pleasures as sugar and liquor once they had been tasted. And guns and knives became essential to the Indians' very survival. Many tribes came to be at the mercy of the trader, as reflected in this 1743 plea to a Hudson's Bay dealer named Isham, who copied down the chief's words in his journal.

You told me last year to bring many Indians. You see I have not lied. Here is a great many young men come with me. Use them kindly! Use them kindly I say! Give them good goods, give them good goods I say!

We lived hard last winter and in want, the [gun] powder being short measure and bad, I say. Tell your servants to fill the measure and not to put their fingers within the brim. Take pity on us, I say!

We come a long way to see you. The French sends for us but we will not go there. We love the English. Give us good black tobacco, moist and hard twisted. Let us see it before opened.

Take pity of us, take pity of us, I say! The guns are bad. Let us trade light guns small in the hand, and well shaped, with locks that will not freeze in the winter. . . .

Let the young men have roll tobacco cheap, kettles thick and high for the shape and size, strong ears [handle loops], and the baile [handle] to lap [fall] just upon the side.

Give us good measure in cloth. Let us see the old measures. Do you mind me!

The young man loves you by coming to see you, take pity, take pity I say! And give them good, they love to dress and be fine. Do you understand me!

ANONYMOUS, *Tribe unknown*

· 4 ·

You Rot the Guts
of Our Young Men

Distilled liquor was the bane of Indian existence everywhere, wrecking family life, causing humiliating sprees of self-destruction, and insidiously used by corrupt whites to confuse Indians before trade or land negotiations. Here a mid-seventeenth-century chieftain of the Catawbas—a large tribe inhabiting the Carolinas—scolds North Carolina authorities with a complaint frequently expressed by Indian leaders. Known as King Haglar by English colonists, the chief spoke these words on August 29, 1754. Although he continued to petition for years for an em-

bargo on firewater, by the close of the eighteenth century liquor, along with successive epidemics of smallpox and attacks by the Iroquois, had decimated his people.

Brothers, here is one thing you yourselves are to blame very much in; that is you rot your grain in tubs, out of which you take and make strong spirits.

You sell it to our young men and give it [to] them, many times; they get very drunk with it [and] this is the very cause that they oftentimes commit those crimes that is offensive to you and us and all through the effect of that drink. It is also very bad for our people, for it rots their guts and causes our men to get very sick and many of our people has lately died by the effects of that strong drink, and I heartily wish you would do something to prevent your people from daring to sell or give them any of that strong drink, upon any consideration whatever, for that will be a great means of our being free from being accused of those crimes that is committed by our young men and will prevent many of the abuses that is done by them through the effects of that strong drink.

KING HAGLAR, *Catawba*

· 5 ·

Some Strange Animal

The "sky dogs," as the people of the far western plains called horses, inspired a cultural revolution. Suddenly tribes could cut their hunting time by a significant fraction and roam great distances to trade and raid. The costume art of the Plains Indian blossomed. Tepees became taller, and their furnishings very elaborate. Ceremonies increased in complexity. Personal wealth was tallied in mounts.

Whereas in 1730 the southern Blackfoot were relatively defenseless against attacks by mounted northern Shoshoni, three generations later they had become the lords of the northern Plains. Around the turn of the nineteenth century, Wolf Calf, a Piegan—the southernmost of the three Blackfoot tribes—told the Plains Indian scholar George Bird Grinnell this story of the tribe's first sight of horses and of a chief whose name appropriately changed from Dog to Many Horses.

The first horses we ever saw came from west of the mountains. A band of the Piegans were camped on Belly River, at a place that we call "Smash the Heads," where we jumped buffalo. They had been driving buffalo over the cliff here, so that they had plenty of meat.

There had come over the mountains to hunt buffalo a Kutenai who had some horses, and he was running buffalo; but for some reason he had no luck. He could kill nothing. He had seen from far off the Piegan camp, but he did not go near it, for the Piegans and the Kutenais were enemies.

This Kutenai could not kill anything, and he and his family had nothing to eat and were starving. At last he made up his mind that he would go into the camp of his enemies and give himself up, for he said, "I might as well be killed at once as die of hunger." So with his wife and children he rode away from his camp up in the mountains, leaving his lodge standing and his horses feeding about it, all except those which his woman and his three children were riding, and started for the camp of the Piegans.

They had just made a big drive, and had run a great lot of

buffalo over the cliff. There were many dead in the pískun [corral] and the men were killing those that were left alive, when suddenly the Kutenai, on his horse, followed by his wife and children on theirs, rode over a hill near by. When they saw him, all the Piegans were astonished and wondered what this could be. None of them had ever seen anything like it, and they were afraid. They thought it was something mysterious. The chief of the Piegans called out to his people: "This is something very strange. I have heard of wonderful things that have happened from the earliest times until now, but I never heard of anything like this. This thing must have come from above (i.e., from the sun), or else it must have come out of the hill (i.e., from the earth). Do not do anything to it; be still and wait. If we try to hurt it, may be it will ride into that hill again, or may be something bad will happen. Let us wait."

As it drew nearer, they could see that it was a man coming, and that he was on some strange animal. The Piegans wanted their chief to go toward him and speak to him. The chief did not wish to do this; he was afraid; but at last he started to go to meet the Kutenai, who was coming. When he got near to him, the Kutenai made signs that he was friendly, and patted his horse on his neck and made signs to the chief. "I give you this animal." The chief made signs that he was friendly, and the Kutenai rode into the camp and were received as friends, and food was given them and they ate, and their hunger was satisfied.

The Kutenai stayed with these Piegans for some time, and the Kutenai man told the chief that he had more horses at his camp up in the mountains, and that beyond the mountains there were plenty of horses. The Piegan said, "I have never heard of a man riding an animal like this." He asked the Kutenai to bring in the rest of his horses; and one night he started out, and the next day came back driving all his horses before him, and they came to the camp, and all the people saw them and looked at them and wondered. . . .

This young man . . . finally became head chief of the Piegans. His name at first was Dog, and afterward Sits-in-the-Middle, and at last Many Horses. He had so many horses he could not keep track of them all. After he had so many horses, he would select ten boys out of each band of the Piegans to care for his horses. Many Horses had more horses than all the rest of the tribe. Many Horses died a good many years ago. These were the first horses the Piegans saw.

When they first got horses, the people did not know what they fed on. They would offer the animals pieces of dried meat, or would take a piece of backfat and rub their noses with it, to try to get them to eat it. Then the horses would turn away and put down their heads, and begin to eat the grass of the prairie. . . .

White people had begun to come into this country, and Many Horses' young men wanted ropes and iron arrowpoints and saddle blankets, and the people were beginning to kill furs and skins to trade. Many Horses began to trade with his own people for these things. He would ask the young men of the tribe to kill skins for him, and they would bring them to him and he would give them a horse or two in exchange. Then he would send his relations in to the Hudson's Bay post to trade, but he would never go himself. The white men wanted to see him, and sent word to him to come in, but he would never do so.

At length, one winter, these white men packed their dog sledges with goods and started to see Many Horses. They took with them guns. The Piegans heard that the whites were coming, and Many Horses sent word to all the people to come together and meet him at a certain place, where the whites were coming. When these came to the camp, they asked where Many Horses' lodge was, and the people pointed out to them the Crow painted lodge. The whites went to this lodge and began to unpack their things—guns, clothing, knives, and goods of all kinds.

Many Horses sent two men to go in different directions through the camp and ask all the principal men, young and old, to come together to his lodge. They all came. Some went in and some sat outside. Then these white men began to distribute the guns, and with each gun they gave a bundle of powder and ball. At this same time, the young men received white blankets and the old men black coats. Then we first got knives, and the white men showed us how to use knives; to split down the legs and rip up the belly—to skin for trade.

WOLF CALF, *Piegan*

· 6 ·

Buttocks Bags and Green Coffee Bread

In this humorous story from the Jicarilla Apache of northern New Mexico, the "white people" referred to are probably not the Spanish, who set up a mission among the Jicarilla in the mid-eighteenth century, but the Americans. In 1854, United States troops quelled the Jicarilla marauders, but in 1878, some warriors took to cattle rustling again. In 1887, the tribe was placed on the northern New Mexico reservation where they live today as successful cattle ranchers.

When the white people first came to this country, they gave the Indians hats, pants, shoes, and coats. Dishes and blankets were also given out, and food, such as flour, sugar, and coffee.

These foolish people received some too. They heard the other people say "buttocks bag" [pants were called *tlatsizis*, "buttocks bag"], and they asked, "What is this bag for? What do you put in it?"

"Why, you throw your buttocks in it," was the answer.

So they decided to do it. They put the pants in a low place and got up on a cliff above them. They hopped in place, getting ready to jump. Then they tried to get in the pants. Their feet missed, and they fell. Then they tied the pants around themselves, but the leg part hung down behind. Some put the pants on backward; some had the legs hanging down in front. That's the way they went around. They put the shirts on. Some wore them in the right way; some put them on backward. The hats they used for carrying water. They didn't know what hats were for. They thought a hat was some kind of dipper. They didn't know what all those things were.

They wouldn't keep gloves. They said, "This must be Bear's hand." The shoes they wouldn't keep either. "These must be the bear's moccasins," they said.

They didn't know what flour was either. They just threw it away. They kept nothing but the sack and emptied out the flour. All the Indians did this, even those who were not foolish. And the baking powder they threw away too.

At first they tried to eat bacon. They made soup of it and ate too much of it. A lot of them died from eating it.

At first they tried to make the flour into a mush. They tried to use it like cornmeal. But it was too sticky, and they threw it away. The brown sugar they liked though. Some of the children ate it like candy. They tasted the salt. They knew what that was. The white people gave them beans too. The beans they recognized. They knew how to eat them.

They were all given green coffee. This is what all the Apaches

One of the most long-lasting trading posts, Lorenzo Hubbell's, in Ganado, Arizona. (MUSEUM OF NEW MEXICO)

did with it, not just the foolish ones. They boiled the green beans for two days. They didn't get any softer. The people couldn't eat it. So they pounded it up and thought they would make a mush of it. It didn't taste good even though they stirred sugar into it. So they tried to make bread of it after grinding it. That didn't taste good either. They gave it up then and threw it away.

ANONYMOUS, *Jicarilla Apache*

· 7 ·

The Bewitched Pale Man

Because the Dogrib people of Canada had to cross the terrain of their greatest enemy, the Maskegon Indians, in order to trade with the French, they conducted their business with the Hudson's Bay Company instead. This tale was recited by Vital Thomas, a contemporary Dogrib storyteller from Rae, near Marten Lake in central Canada.

Fort Simpson is an old, old fort. In the fall, the Dogribs used to go to Simpson to trade. One time, one bunch went on ahead of another bunch by four or five days. When they got to Simpson, the Hudson's Bay manager wouldn't give them any credit. He was mad at them. He said "You guys haven't paid me from last year. I won't give you a thing." Those poor Indians, there was nothing they could do but go back. They were one day out from the fort when they met the other bunch coming along to trade. They said to the other bunch, "There is no use going on, you might as well turn back. The Hudson's Bay man won't give us credit. There is nothing there for you."

There was an old fellow with the second bunch. He was Seretton's father—not that Seretton who is living here now but another one. That old man listened to all the talking, and then he said to his bunch, "Well, we might as well go on in and see what it is like. We can't turn back now." That night when they made camp, those fellows asked the old man if he couldn't change the Hudson's Bay man's mind, because they had come from a long, long way, from Snare Lake or Indin Lake maybe.

They offered to pay the old man, so finally he said, "I'll do the best I can to change his mind."

So the old man started to sing, "Hey hey, Pale Man! hey hey." And he started to work his arms down into the earth. Finally he was down into the earth about halfway up his arms. He was still singing, "Hey hey, Pale Man!" when he said, "Here is the man we have been talking about," and he brought the Hudson's Bay man up out of the ground as far as his armpits. Then he began to rub his hands over the Hudson's Bay man's head as if he was pulling or cupping up water. All of a sudden he clapped his hands loudly and said, "Here it is! I got his mind right here in my hands!" And the Hudson's Bay man sank back through the earth. "He has gone home now without his mind. We got to hurry to get there. We got to do our trading fast and go right back because I can't hold his mind very long."

They started out early and got to Simpson about the middle of the day. When they went in the store, the Hudson's Bay man acted like he was dreaming, kind of like he was asleep. The Dog-ribs started to ask for things. And that trader gave them every-thing they asked for, just like he was half drunk. They got everything they could think of on credit. And then the old man said to them, "We might as well go home now. I can't hold it any longer." And as soon as they got back into the bush, the old medicine man sent the Bay man back his mind.

VITAL THOMAS, *Dogrib*

BEARERS OF
THE CROSS

To Native American peoples the land they inhabited was sacred, sanctified. Most of them conceived of the earth and heavens as a cosmic temple. Many tribes could point to the exact cave or hill or lake from whence, according to their mythology, they as a people had first emerged from an ancient underworld. The surrounding trees, plants, seas, rivers, deserts, animals, and other forms of wildlife all figured as supernatural forces in their legends. Above was the canopy of Father Sky; below, the enduring body of Mother Earth.

Their spiritual reference points were prominent environmental landmarks. In Arizona the Navajo universe was bounded by four sacred peaks. A hundred miles to the east, the San Juan Pueblo's world was circumscribed by four different sacred mountains. Everywhere tribes enshrined caves, springs, mesas, and lakes, leaving prayer sticks and food offerings for the spirits there. They felt toward these natural landmarks as a Taos woman spoke of Blue Lake: "I think of it as an altar."

Many Native American peoples cherished a belief in a Golden Age when men and animals had lived and talked together as

Tonajinni (Blanca Peak), one of the four sacred mountains of the Navajo.
(LAURA GILPIN)

brothers. Northwest Coast families proudly proclaimed their descent from the eagle, the raven, and the wolf. Medicine men in nearly every tribe were initiated into their roles as mystical healers and prophets by animal instructors who had appeared to them in visions. Through elaborate ceremonies refined over centuries, young Indian men and women learned how to revere the sacred forces of the living, natural world. The yearning for a dimly remembered time of wholeness, when man lived in peaceful harmony with all of nature, was inherent in their highest rituals as well as in the activities of their everyday lives.

"The old people came literally to love the soil," wrote the Sioux author Luther Standing Bear. "They sat on the ground with the feeling of being close to a mothering power. It was good for the skin to touch the earth, and the old people liked to remove their moccasins and walk with their bare feet on the sacred earth. The soil was soothing, strengthening, cleansing and healing."

When white men first witnessed Indians impersonating animal spirits in costume and dance, and worshiping rocks and rainbows, they failed to see this as a form of deep religious expression. To their Christian minds, these were deplorable pagan rites. Worship of more than one deity, and sacrificial offerings directed at the natural world, stamped Indians as a misguided, lesser form of mankind. Here were Christless heathens crying to be rescued from eternal damnation.

For their part most Native Americans were not averse initially to Christianity. Before the white man appeared, tribes had absorbed new waves of religious thought. To them a fresh form of worship did not negate the old. The great value they placed on their own traditional beliefs made them especially curious about the magical deeds of this new medicine man, the Son of God. They were courteous listeners even when they did not understand a word of a missionary's preaching. They were fearful, too. For a people so aggressive and determined as the whites must have powerful gods. But this openheartedness did not always satisfy the missionaries. Their insistence upon an exclusive devotion to one God, and the criticism meted out when their Indian converts disappointed them, caused centuries of conflict. For not many Indians were about to repudiate their own traditional religions. Even when Christianity forced their children to doubt the old ways, they devised new religious ceremonies blending both Christian and Indian concepts and symbolism to keep their heritage alive.

The first missionaries came from Spain. Traveling in partnership with the conquistadors, these Roman Catholic padres belonged to the Dominican, Jesuit, Franciscan, and Augustinian orders. In Florida, in the Southwest, and in California they created self-sufficient missions where Indians were to live, worship, and work away from tribal influences. The native converts were trained to tend fruit orchards and grow crops, graze sheep and cattle, read and chant holy scripture, and develop their skill as craftsmen in weaving, leatherwork, blacksmithing, and in the manufacture of olive oil and soap.

Stern with their Indian "children," the padres depended on soldiers garrisoned at each mission to round up neophytes, as newly baptized Indians were known. Each night the Native American men and women were locked into separate dormitories. The Spanish soldiers flogged runaways and those found secretly practicing tribal rites; they quelled the frequent rebellions against strict mission discipline.

But some priests, caught between the prevalent attitude toward Indians and their own consciences, protected their converts. The Native American's earliest white champion was a Spanish missionary, Father Bartolome de Las Casas. Published in 1544, his proposed *New Laws For The Indies* pleaded for an end to Indian peonage. Later mission priests were often forced to shield their converts when silver-mine bosses or large ranchers tried to conscript them for cheap labor.

By 1635 more than forty thriving Spanish missions had been established in Florida. They lasted for another hundred years until British soldiers from the north, with their Creek and Catawba allies, destroyed them and sold thousands of Indian converts into slavery.

The most durable missions lay in the Southwest. But there Christianity was eventually forced to an accommodation with traditional Indian ritual. By 1633, following an intensive construction campaign of adobe-and-timber churches among the Zuñi, Hopi, and other Pueblos, sixty thousand Indians had been baptized, and ninety chapels were scattered throughout seven missionary districts. Mass was compulsory. Natives who practiced their traditional ceremonies were beaten or executed. Such oppression against this proud and sophisticated people finally led to the famous Pueblo Rebellion of 1680, when all the Spanish missions were destroyed and those priests and colonists who survived were driven south across the Rio Grande into Mexico. When the government of New Spain reconquered the region twelve years later, the churches were rebuilt, and Catholic priests still serve in some of them today. But hereafter both Christ and the kachinas—the masked gods of Pueblo religion—were worshiped in a unique mixture of indigenous and imported ritual.

In California the first Spanish mission was erected on July 16, 1769, near the present-day site of San Diego. Over the next fifty years Native American labor constructed twenty more missions northward along the Pacific Coast to San Francisco. But after 1826, having won its independence from Spain, the Mexican government began ordering the padres to abandon their churches. Although the intention was that the land should be distributed among the Indians who had come to rely on the missions for food and shelter, it wound up in private hands. The Mission Indians were generally evicted, left without livelihood and ill prepared to return to their former mountain hamlets. Between 1769 and 1830 disease, brutality, and drastic dietary changes, particularly affecting the Mission Indian population, had reduced the coastal Native American population from seventy thousand to twenty-four thousand Indians. By 1840 only six thousand Mission Indians were left, eking out their livelihood as serfs on large ranches.

In New France, Jesuits often accompanied the trader-explorers opening up river routes, men like Père Marquette, who traveled with Louis Jolliet on his 1673 voyage down "the Great Water" (the Mississippi River). The Jesuits baptized tribesmen in northeastern Canada and the Mississippi Valley. Generally they were humane and tended to adjust to the natives' way of life. In northern New England, for example, a French Jesuit named Sebastian Rale lived alone among the Abnaki Indians for thirty-four years, speaking their language and fighting by their side against the British.

In the British colonies, however, the Protestant clergy was more disposed to ignore or damn the Indians than to proselytize them. There were rare individuals like the Rhode Island minister Roger Williams, who spoke out on behalf of religious freedom and land rights for the Narraganset Indians. But extremist seventeenth-century Protestant leaders—like the Puritan preacher Cotton Mather—considered Indians "agents of Satan."

English-speaking missionaries dispatched Indian converts far and wide to deliver in broken English testimonials of salvation from alcohol and savagery, but they rarely collected sizable native congregations. Not until the late eighteenth century did Protestant proselytizing gain any significant momentum. By then the great aim of numerous Protestant missionary societies was to "civilize" the Indians. Native American boys and girls were indoctrinated into the "gospel of soap" and the ethics of hard work, personal sacrifice, and economic independence. In 1865 the United States government formalized an arrangement whereby Protestant groups would administer the government-owned Indian boarding schools. Their efforts did more to crush Indianness than any other missionary campaign.

A baptismal font carved by a Tsimshian artist from the Northwest Coast.
(THE MUSEUM OF ANTHROPOLOGY, UNIVERSITY OF BRITISH COLUMBIA, VANCOUVER)

Since in traditional Indian life, religious ritual permeated nearly every political, social, and economic activity, the message of most Christian missionaries was that Indians had to reject all aspects of their own culture. The following selections reflect in some measure the range of tribal response to this requirement, from acceptance by the California Luiseño to rebellion by the New Mexican Pueblos to adoption of a blend of old and new religious beliefs as described by the Kiowa-Apache, Jim Whitewolf.

· 1 ·

Burn the Temples,
Break Up the Bells

The Pueblo Rebellion of 1680, incited by eighty years of cruelty to Native Americans in the Southwest, caught the Spanish completely off guard. Within a matter of weeks, over four hundred of them were massacred. Priests were slain before their altars; the mission churches and livestock were put to the torch; and twenty-five hundred soldiers were driven south to Mexico.

In an effort to discover how such an attack could possibly have occurred, Spanish inquisitors interrogated Indian prisoners, among them Pedro Naranjo of the San Felipe Pueblo. This excerpt from Naranjo's replies to his questioners describes how Popé, a San Juan medicine man and the leader of the "Indian sorcerers" mentioned in Naranjo's statement, received spiritual guidance for the rebellion. As its main strategist, he prepared the secret timing by which all nineteen of the Rio Grande Pueblos rose up in arms simultaneously.

[Under oath, Pedro Naranjo declared that the Indians] have planned to rebel on various occasions through conspiracies of the Indian sorcerers, and that although in some pueblos the messages were accepted, in other parts they would not agree to it, and that it is true that during the government of the said señor general seven or eight Indians were hanged for this same cause, whereupon the unrest subsided. . . .

Finally, in the past years, at the summons of an Indian named Popé who is said to have communication with the devil, it happened that in an estufa [sacred meeting place or *kiva*] of the pueblo of Los Taos there appeared to the said Popé three figures of Indians who never came out of the estufa. They gave the said Popé to understand that they were going underground to the lake of Copala. He saw these figures emit fire from all the extremities of their bodies, and that one of them was called Caudi, another Tilini, and the other Tleume; and these three beings spoke to the said Popé, who was in hiding from the secretary, Francisco Xavier, who wished to punish him as a sorcerer.

They told him to make a cord of maguey fiber and tie some knots in it which would signify the number of days that they must wait for the rebellion. He said that the cord was passed through all the pueblos of the kingdom so that those which agreed to it [the rebellion] might untie one knot in sign of obedience. . . . As a sign of agreement and notice of having concurred in the treason and perfidy they were to send up smoke signals to that effect in each one of the pueblos singly. The said cord was taken from pueblo to pueblo by the swiftest youths under the penalty of death if they revealed the secret.

Everything being thus arranged, two days before the time set for its execution, because his lordship had learned of it and had imprisoned two Indian accomplices from the pueblo of Tesuque, it was carried out prematurely that night, because it seemed to them that they were now discovered; and they killed religious, Spaniards, women, and children. . . .

Finally the señor governor and those who were with him escaped from the siege, and later this declarant saw that as soon as the Spaniards had left the kingdom an order came from the said Indian, Popé, in which he commanded all the Indians to break the lands and enlarge their cultivated fields, saying that now they were as they had been in ancient times, free from the labor they had performed for the religious and the Spaniards, who could not now be alive. . . .

Asked for what reason they so blindly burned the images, temples, crosses, and other things of divine worship, he [Pedro Naranjo] stated that the said Indian, Popé, came down in person, and with him El Saca and El Chato from the pueblo of Los Taos, and other captains and leaders and many people who were in his train, and he ordered in all the pueblos through which he passed that they instantly break up and burn the images of the holy Christ, the Virgin Mary and the other saints, the crosses, and everything pertaining to Christianity, and that they burn the temples, break up the bells, and separate from the wives whom God had given them in marriage and take those whom they desired.

In order to take away their baptismal names, the water, and the holy oils, they were to plunge into the rivers and wash themselves with amole, which is a root native to the country, washing even their clothing, with the understanding that there would thus be taken from them the character of the holy sacraments. . . . He saw to it that they at once erected and rebuilt their houses of idolatry which they call estufas, and made very ugly masks in imitation of the devil in order to dance the dance of the cacina [kachina]; and he said likewise that the devil had given them to understand that living thus in accordance with the law of their ancestors, they would harvest a great deal of maize, many beans, a great abundance of cotton, calabashes, and very large watermelons and cantaloupes; and that they could erect their houses and enjoy abundant health and leisure. . . .

PEDRO NARANJO, *San Felipe Pueblo*

· 2 ·
A Good Indian's Dilemma

Even when an Indian was baptized as "the black robes"—missionaries—insisted, racial bigotry kept him from gaining fuller acceptance by whites. The Fox or Mesquakie Indians of the southern Great Lakes region provide this ironic anecdote about a convert's can't-win plight.

Once there was an Indian who became a Christian. He became a very good Christian; he went to church, and he didn't smoke or drink, and he was good to everyone. He was a very good man. Then he died. First he went to the Indian hereafter, but they wouldn't take him because he was a Christian. Then he went to Heaven, but they wouldn't let him in—because he was an Indian. Then he went to Hell, but they wouldn't admit him there either, because he was so good. So he came alive again, and he went to the Buffalo Dance and the other dances and taught his children to do the same thing.

ANONYMOUS, *Fox*

· 3 ·
We Never Quarrel About Religion

In this excerpt from a famous speech delivered in 1828, the Iroquois leader Red Jacket replies to a representative of the Boston Missionary Society named Mr. Cram. The missionary had asked for approval to spread his faith among tribes within the Iroquois sphere of influence in northern New York State. When the meeting was over, Cram refused to shake the Indians' outstretched hands. There could be no fellowship between the religion of God and the works of the devil, he announced. The Iroquois are said to have smiled.

Friend and Brother! It was the will of the Great Spirit that we should meet together this day. He orders all things, and he has given us a fine day for our council. He has taken his garment from before the sun, and caused it to shine with brightness upon us. Our eyes are opened that we see clearly. Our ears are unstopped that we have been able to hear distinctly the words you have spoken. For all these favors we thank the Great Spirit, and him only. . . .

Brother! Continue to listen. You say that you are sent to instruct us how to worship the Great Spirit agreeably to his mind; and if we do not take hold of the religion which you white people teach, we shall be unhappy hereafter. You say that you are right and we are lost. How do we know this to be true? We understand that your religion is written in a book. If it was intended for us as well as for you, why has not the Great Spirit given it to us; and not only to us, but why did he not give to our forefathers the knowledge of that book, with the means of understanding it rightly? We only know what you tell us about it. How shall we know when to believe, being so often deceived by the white people?

Brother! You say there is but one way to worship and serve the Great Spirit. If there is but one religion, why do you white people differ so much about it? Why do not all agree, as you can all read the book?

Brother! We do not understand these things. We are told that your religion was given to your forefathers, and has been handed down from father to son. We also have a religion which was given to our forefathers, and has been handed down to us their children. We worship that way. It teacheth us to be thankful for all the favors we receive, to love each other, and to be united. We never quarrel about religion. . . .

RED JACKET, *Iroquois*

· 4 ·

Janitin Is Named *Jesús*

Sometime between 1820 and 1830, a Kamia Indian named Janitin was brought under guard to the San Miguel Mission in California, south of San Diego. As an old man in the year 1878, he told an interviewer what he had experienced at the mission and displayed the scars he had received at the hands of the Dominican fathers. Not all Spanish priests behaved so harshly. Some Franciscans in the Southwest were actually welcomed by the Indians, because in the natives' own words, "These go about poorly dressed and barefooted like us; they eat what we eat,

*they settle down among us, and their intercourse is gentle." But
the success of the California padres was judged by the number
of Indian names on their baptismal rolls and the amount of
farm and craft goods produced at the missions. That called for
fresh crews of Indian laborers.*

I and two of my relatives went down from the Sierra of Neji
to the beach of el Rosarito, to catch clams for eating and to carry
to the sierra as we were accustomed to do all the years; we did
no harm to anyone on the road, and on the beach we thought
of nothing more than catching and drying clams in order to
carry them to our village.

While we were doing this, we saw two men on horseback coming rapidly towards us; my relatives were immediately afraid
and they fled with all speed, hiding themselves in a very dense
willow grove which then existed in the canyon of the Rancho
del Rosarito.

As soon as I saw myself alone, I also became afraid of those
men and ran to the forest in order to join my companions, but
already it was too late, because in a moment they overtook me
and lassoed and dragged me for a long distance, wounding me
much with the branches over which they dragged me, pulling
me lassoed as I was with their horses running; after this they
roped me with my arms behind and carried me off to the Mission
of San Miguel, making me travel almost at a run in order to keep
up with their horses, and when I stopped a little to catch my
wind, they lashed me with the lariats that they carried, making
me understand by signs that I should hurry; after much traveling
in this manner, they diminished the pace and lashed me in order
that I would always travel at the pace of the horses.

When we arrived at the mission, they locked me in a room
for a week; the father [a Dominican priest] made me go to his

habitation and he talked to me by means of an interpreter, telling me that he would make me a Christian, and he told me many things that I did not understand, and Cunnur, the interpreter, told me that I should do as the father told me, because now I was not going to be set free, and it would go very bad with me if I did not consent in it. They gave me *atole de mayz* [corn gruel] to eat which I did not like because I was not accustomed to that food; but there was nothing else to eat.

One day they threw water on my head and gave me salt to eat, and with this the interpreter told me that now I was Christian and that I was called *Jesús*: I knew nothing of this, and I tolerated it all because in the end I was a poor Indian and did not have recourse but to conform myself and tolerate the things they did with me.

The following day after my baptism, they took me to work with the other Indians, and they put me to cleaning a *milpa* [cornfield] of maize; since I did not know how to manage the hoe that they gave me, after hoeing a little, I cut my foot and could not continue working with it, but I was put to pulling out the weeds by hand, and in this manner I did not finish the task that they gave me. In the afternoon they lashed me for not finishing the job, and the following day the same thing happened as on the previous day. Every day they lashed me unjustly because I did not finish what I did not know how to do, and thus I existed for many days until I found a way to escape; but I was tracked and they caught me like a fox; there they seized me by lasso as on the first occasion, and they carried me off to the mission torturing me on the road. After we arrived, the father passed along the corridor of the house, and he ordered that they fasten me to the stake and castigate me; they lashed me until I lost consciousness, and I did not regain consciousness for many hours afterwards. For several days I could not raise myself from the floor where they had laid me, and I still have on my shoulders the marks of the lashes which they gave me then.

JANITIN, *Kamia*

· 5 ·

The Freedom to Work

When he was about thirteen years old, a Luiseño Indian named Pablo Tac related this fond and rare firsthand reminiscence of life at the Mission of San Luis Rey de Francia, at one time the largest of the Spanish missions in California. In 1822, twenty-four years after the mission was founded, Tac became the 3,896th Indian child to be baptized there. His depiction of its daily activities nicely fits the Spanish missionary's dream of how mission life should flow. Tac was such an exemplary pupil that the mission's founder took him to Rome and enrolled him in Urban College. There he died of disease just before he turned twenty. The industrious work of the Indian "neophytes" at San Luis Rey de Francia was short-lived; after 1834 the mission was abandoned.

The god who was adored at that time was the sun and the fire. Thus we lived among the woods until merciful God freed us of these miseries through Father Antonio Peyri, a Catalan, who arrived in our country in the afternoon with seven Spanish soldiers.

When the missionary arrived in our country with a small troop, our captain and also the others were astonished, seeing them from afar, but they did not run away or seize arms to kill them, but having sat down, they watched them. But when they drew near, then the captain got up (for he was seated with the others) and met them. They halted, and the missionary then began to speak, the captain saying perhaps in his language, "*Hichsom iva haluon, pulluchajam cham quinai.*" "What is it that you seek here? Get out of our country!" But they did not understand him, and they answered him in Spanish, and the captain began with signs, and the Fernandino [missionary], understanding him, gave him gifts and in this manner made him his friend. . . .

The Fernandino Father remains in our country with the little troop that he brought. A camp was made, and here he lived for many days. In the morning he said Mass, and then he planned how he would baptize them, where he would put his house, the church, and as there were five thousand souls (who were all the Indians there were), how he would sustain them, and seeing how it could be done. Having the captain for his friend, he was afraid of nothing. . . .

He [Father Peyri] ordered the Indians to carry stone from the sea (which is not far) for the foundations, to make bricks, roof tiles, to cut beams, reeds, and what was necessary. They did it with the masters who were helping them, and within a few years they finished working. They made a church with three altars for all the neophytes (the great altar is nearly all gilded), two chapels, two sacristies, two choirs, a flower garden for the church, a high tower with five bells, two small and three large, the cemetery with a crucifix in the middle for all those who die here. . . .

The Fernandino Father, as he was alone and very accustomed to the usages of the Spanish soldiers, seeing that it would be very difficult for him alone to give orders to that people, and, moreover, people that had left the woods just a few years before, therefore appointed alcaldes [official leaders] from the people themselves that knew how to speak more Spanish than the others and were better than the others in their customs. There were

Luiseño women at the crumbling San Luis Rey Mission, once the richest of California's missions. (LOS ANGELES COUNTY MUSEUM OF NATURAL HISTORY)

seven of these alcaldes, with rods as a symbol that they could judge the others. . . . In the afternoon, the alcaldes gather at the house of the missionary. They bring news of that day, and if the missionary tells them something that all the people of the country ought to know, they return to the villages shouting, "Tomorrow morning. . . ."

Returning to the villages, each one of the alcaldes wherever he goes cries out what the missionary has told them, in his language, and all the country hears it. "Tomorrow the sowing begins and so the laborers go to the chicken yard and assemble there." And again he goes saying these same words until he reaches his own village to eat something and then to sleep. In the morning you will see the laborers appear in the chicken yard and assemble there according to what they heard last night.

With the laborers goes a Spanish majordomo and others, neophyte alcaldes to see how the work is done, to hurry them if they are lazy, so that they will soon finish what was ordered, and to punish the guilty or lazy one who leaves his plow and quits the field keeping on with his laziness. They work all day, but not always. At noon they leave work, and then they bring them *posole*. (*Posole* is what the Spaniards of California call maize in hot water.) They eat it with gusto, and they remain sated until afternoon when they return to their villages. The shoemakers work making chairs, leather knapsacks, reins and shoes for the cowboys, neophytes, majordomos and Spanish soldiers, and when they have finished, they bring and deliver them to the missionary to give to the cowboys. The blacksmiths make bridle kits, keys, bosses for bridles, nails for the church, and all work for all. . . .

In the Mission of San Luis Rey de Francia the Fernandino Father is like a king. He has his pages, alcaldes, majordomos, musicians, soldiers, gardens, ranchos, livestock, horses by the thousand, cows, bulls by the thousand, oxen, mules, asses, 12,000 lambs, 200 goats, etc. There are five gardens that are for all, very large. The Fernandino Father drinks little, and as almost all the gardens produce wine, he who knows the customs of the neophytes well does not wish to give any wine to any of them, but sells it to the English or Anglo-Americans, not for money, but for clothing for the neophytes, linen for the church, hats, muskets, plates, coffee, tea, sugar and other things. The products of the Mission are butter, tallow, hides, chamois leather, bear skins, wine, white wine, brandy, oil, maize, wheat, beans and also bull horns which the English take by the thousand to Boston.

PABLO TAC, *Luiseño*

· 6 ·

A Shaman Obeys

In 1916 Pedro Encinales, one of California's last Salinan Indians, told an anthropologist about this clash between a San Antonio Mission priest and a Native American medicine man. When the Catholic missions in California were finally boarded up in the mid-1830's, Encinales' family, like countless others, clung to the outskirts of the crumbling adobe buildings and the orchards and fields where they once had labored so faithfully. Their plight became a popular philanthropic cause around the turn of the nineteenth century.

Long ago there was an old shaman who had a reputation as a rainmaker who could make rain whenever he wished.

One year there was a long drought and the Padre of the Mission said, "We will test his powers." He gave orders that the old man should be caught and brought before him. Then he said to him, "If you do not make it rain so that it will fill these barrels I will have you tied and whipped."

"It is good," replied the shaman, "I will try." Then he sang. Soon the sky became overcast with clouds and it thundered. Then came the rain furiously; it did not delay long. The barrels which the Padre had placed were filled quickly. Then he told the man to stop the rain. And it stopped. "We do not wish any more," he said. "No, there is enough already!"

PEDRO ENCINALES, *Salinan*

· 7 ·

Always Give Blessings
and Be Thankful

Jim Whitewolf, a Kiowa Apache of southwestern Oklahoma, was born around 1878. In his autobiography he implicitly compares Christian values as he acquired them from missionaries with the Kiowa Apache code of conduct handed down by his grandfather. Unlike the tribes with whom they were most closely associated—the Cheyenne, Arapaho, and Kiowa, who were practically their brothers—the Kiowa Apache had a reputation for friendliness toward whites.

When I was still pretty small, I remember that east of the Agency near Anadarko, there were some Catholic sisters sitting under an arbor in the camp. Someone was calling out to us to come over there because they had something to tell us. My mother and father took me over there. A fellow was there, named Bill Brownbear, who was interpreting for the Catholic sisters. There was another man with those sisters. This man who was with the sisters prayed, and then there was singing. He took out a black book; it was a Bible. He started reading from it. I didn't understand it at that time. The only thing he was doing that I knew was good was the praying because we had always had praying in the Indian way. Every now and then I could understand a little bit, like when he talked about "our Father," but the rest of the time I didn't know what he was talking about.

When the service was over, they said that they would give some of us rosaries. They said that next time they came back they would give out more of them. The men got larger rosaries than the children got. I didn't get any, but my father did. Every two weeks we went to the camp for rations. We went back there again one time—I think it was on Sunday. They had church and went through the same thing as the first time. Then one of the sisters went through the crowd and gave out rosaries. That time I got one. They told me to wear mine all the time. I felt proud of it. I never took it off. I wore it when I slept and even when I went in swimming. People would go back to that service every Sunday, but they went just to get a rosary with beads on the chain. A lot of them didn't even believe in it, but they wanted those beads. I guess those Catholics went around to the Kiowas, too.

The next thing I knew was that the missionary, Mr. Methvin, was building a church right north of the old Agency. I saw them working on that building. After it was finished, they went around and told people that, when they heard the bell, they should come over there. The people around camp were talking about how this

Jesuits were known for seeking out Indians where they lived. Here, a Father Crimont, S.J., visits the Crow Indians in 1890.

(WESTERN HISTORY COLLECTIONS, UNIVERSITY OF OKLAHOMA LIBRARY)

man was going to show them how they could come back after they died. They thought that he was some kind of a medicine man. What he meant was that, if you led a good life, your soul would have eternal life. But the Indians thought that he could bring the dead back to life. Everybody started sending their children to that church. My mother told me that, if I should die, I wouldn't be gone forever but would come back to life. This all happened before I ever went to school.

Another boy and I went to church one time. The preacher was talking and there was a Kiowa fellow alongside him interpreting. Then they divided us up into groups and gave us each a little paper. After that I went to church all the time. Soon some of the older people started to come to church. Later on I began to understand that they meant that when you die you don't return to earth but go up to heaven.

Years after that, I heard that they were going to build another church down by Cache Creek. Then some white people came there. Mr. Curtis came there. Some of us helped haul rocks to build this church. On Sundays Mr. Curtis would come out to where we were camping and talk to us. This was before the church was finished. Bill Brownbear was interpreting for them. Some of the Indians started to believe in it. I guess it was because most of them always had believed in praying.

One time Mr. Curtis said that he was going to read us the Ten Commandments. All I got out of it was the one that says, "Thou shalt not steal." I remembered that one. He said that if you stole you wouldn't go to heaven. Henry Brownbear got up and said, "I used to steal horses, but I don't do it any more." Another old man got up and repeated the commandment, "Thou shalt not lie." He said, "I don't lie. I always tell the truth." Henry Brownbear would get up after every commandment that was read and repeat it. His Indian name was "Old Man Nervous." That was because he had a tremor of the hands. He repeated every single commandment. He was the only one who kept jumping up like that. When Mr. Curtis got to the commandment that said you should not go with another man's wife, Henry Brownbear just whistled and said, "That's too much. I want that woman sitting over there. I guess I'll just have to go to hell. . . ."

When I was little I stayed with my grandfather. He was a tall, slim man. My grandfather's cousins used to come. They were all old men. My grandfather would bring them over, just one of them at a time, and they would sleep with me and tell me stories. My grandfather told me that the Indians didn't fight among themselves any more. He told me to be friendly to people and never to steal or lie about anything. He said that in the old days the Apaches used to ride from up near the Kansas line down to Mexico, looking for good hunting grounds. Whenever they met up with the Sioux, there would be a fight. He told me always to get up early in the morning. He said that when I grew up to be a man, always to get up early and feed and water my horses. He said to take care of the horses and keep them fat, because they would take care of me and help me to find something to eat. He told me that now I didn't need to have a fast horse to do fighting, but that he wanted me to take care of my horses so I could use them to farm with, like the white people were doing, so I would have something. He said not to forget to plant corn to feed my horses with, and to eat. He said there were many ways to use corn and that there were going to be many more, and that was why I should never forget to raise it. He said that someday I would have a home of my own and I should always have lots of wood to cook food with. At that time they prayed for wood, because it helped to prepare food for them and it kept them warm. He told me always to give blessings for food and to be thankful for my home.

JIM WHITEWOLF, *Kiowa Apache*

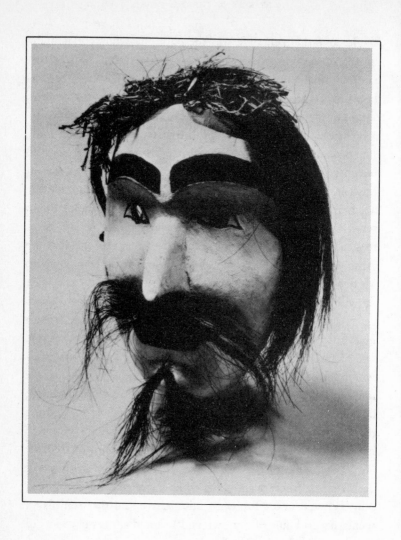

LIVING BESIDE
EACH OTHER

Were red men and white "two distinct races with separate origins and separate destinies," as the Dwamish chief Seattle told the governor of Washington Territory in 1854? Was there no chance for neighborly coexistence between the two peoples?

At first most Atlantic Coast Indians were hospitable to the newcomers, who in return dubbed native chiefs as kings and their wives and sons and daughters as queens, princes, and princesses. With a mixture of courtesy and curiosity, these tribes helped the newcomers stay alive in the wilds. All across the country Indians would become known for harboring non-Indian passersby; they did not inquire if their guests were outlaws or misfits. Nor were they particularly upset when their women bore half-white children; they did not insist on taking white women. "Squaw men"—slang for whites who lived with Indian women—found acceptance among Indians when white society shunned them. If "half-breed" offspring were ostracized from white communities, they always found Indian homes. Growing up bilingual and bicultural, they were well suited to fill the critical frontier

A mask, representing a bearded white man, carved by a Kwakiutl from the Northwest Coast.

roles of intepreter and trader. In the regions marked by Spanish occupation, a *mestizo* class soon arose, mingling the blood of *Indios* and *gente de razón*, or European Spaniards. In Canada intermarriage between French and Indian became so prevalent that it there produced an entirely distinct, mixed-blood group, the Red River *métis*.

But one cannot dream up two more contrary ways of life and systems of belief than those represented by Native American and European societies. The enormous differences in religious values and practices, in the conduct of family and social life, in concepts of property ownership and land use, in traditional attitudes toward work and leisure, made intimacy between Indians and Europeans all too rare. Much of the time they viewed each other as total barbarians. In a talk with Benjamin Franklin, a Delaware tribesman observed, "If a white man in traveling through our country enters one of our cabins, we all treat him as I treat you. We dry him if he is wet, we warm him if he is cold. . . . But if I go into a white man's house in Albany and ask for victuals and drink, they say, 'Get out.' . . . You see they have not learned those little good things we need no meeting to be instructed in because our mothers taught them to us when we were children."

Should an Indian venture inside a white man's home, he often found the etiquette constraining, as an elderly holy man humorously complained to the nineteenth-century missionary Cephus Washburn. "When you come to my cabin I always say to you, 'Go and eat.' . . . But when I come to see you, I never see any food in any of your dwellings; and it is only at certain definite hours that I can find any food; then the bell rattles, ding, ding, ding! and all must go then and eat, or all will soon be out of sight." (Native Americans today still joke about the white man who needs a clock to tell him when he is hungry.)

A major stumbling block between Indians and whites was their opposite attitudes toward the land. In the New World, whites cleared the forests and cultivated the ground, slaughtered wild game in massive quantities, mined the earth's gold and silver as if they would never end, and began peopling villages and towns blocked out after those in their homelands. Yet the Indians viewed themselves as the earth's grateful occupiers and custodians, not as its owners and engineers. Defining land as a commercial product like sugar or gunpowder, the whites measured it, bought it or stole it, fenced it, tilled or built upon it, with an abandon that horrified Indians. At the same time the colonists, whose society was founded on private ownership and consolidation of personal riches, looked disapprovingly at the Indians' custom of sharing land in common.

Such differences in cultural outlook did not lead to problems as long as the colonial presence was limited. Friendship between the two peoples could flower when sensitive whites found themselves in Indian company, and early pioneer families often enjoyed squatting and hunting privileges in Indian territory. In those instances the two peoples had space and time to feel each other out. Moments of peace were also possible when tribal and colonial self-interests overlapped, as with matters of trade.

But the white population increased too rapidly for equilibrium to last. Indians were usually trying to eke out a living on the very lands the burgeoning white population coveted. As eastern forests were thinned of game, stories of white settlements pushing Indians ever westward became commonplace. Tribesmen clinging to ancestral territory suffered racial prejudice and religious intolerance. Whatever fragile understandings had existed were torn asunder in the rush of westward expansion. The main justification for usurping tribal lands, the concept of "right of discovery," had been invented as early as the sixteenth century in Spain. Later explorers customarily claimed vast territories in the name of the monarch or commercial interest who had paid for their ventures. Later, in 1823, the United States Supreme Court upheld the notion that "discovery gave exclusive title to those who made it." And where "right of discovery" did not suffice, right of conquest through armed takeover always would.

Tribes that survived on the outskirts of white communities witnessed their villages torn between pro- and anti-white factions, between "breeches" (pants-wearing Indians who adopted white habits) and "blanket" (traditional) Indians. Despite these wrenching tensions and incessant pressure to choose sides among the embroiled European powers, for the two hundred years of the colonial period most tribes did not consider themselves a conquered people. They held to the vision of retaining their own independent identity. Over the centuries, a theme repeated again and again in tribal speeches is the always reasoned plea that whites recognize the Indians' right to be distinctly themselves. As a Pawnee leader named Petalesharo tried to impress upon President James Monroe in 1822, "He [the Great Spirit] made my skin red and yours white; he placed us on this earth and intended that we should live differently from each other. He made the whites to cultivate the earth, and feed on domestic animals; but he made us, red skins, to rove through the uncultivated woods and plains, to feed on wild animals, to dress in their skins. . . ."

But entreaties to Live and Let Live, no matter how eloquently expressed, usually fell on deaf ears. The white colonists could not keep from looking down upon the Indian, an attitude that did not escape the natives. "Why come the English hither," a Narraganset Indian questioned Roger Williams, "and measuring others by themselves?"

As early as the mid-seventeenth century the British hoped to establish domestic tranquility between colonies by setting aside living space for friendly, usually Christianized Indians. But these prototype reservations still did not solve the question of how to handle the "wild" Indians. Finally, in 1763, the British drew up a proclamation calling for a boundary line between their "civilization" and "Indian Territory"—which was defined as "any lands beyond the heads or sources of any of the rivers which fall into the Atlantic Ocean from the West or Northwest." Yet even the immensity of the great American West was soon insufficient for this separate-but-equal scheme. The Creek chief Speckled Snake summed up the experience of most tribes: "I have listened to a great many talks from our Great Father. But they always began and ended in this—Get a little farther; you are too near me."

In the nineteenth century, most white Americans came to believe that it was God's will for them to rule from sea to shining sea. By and large, neighborly coexistence between Indians and whites was already a dead dream. To the beleaguered western Indians this notion of Manifest Destiny meant the final series of campaigns to wrest from them their birthright, their holy lands. The only destiny they could now pursue was as fugitive or conquered nations.

· 1 ·

Remove the Cause
of Our Uneasiness

During the winter of 1607, the new colonists at Jamestown, Virginia, lost half their number through starvation and disease. Without the help of their Native American neighbors in the Powhatan Confederacy, made up of some thirty tribes, the English would have altogether perished. In this 1609 plea for a con-

tinuation of friendly relations, copied down by Captain John Smith, the sixty-year-old leader of the confederacy Wahunsona-cock—or King Powhatan as he was called by the English—warns of the very abuses that finally drove his people to rise against the Jamestown community. In the spring of 1622, the Indians killed nearly 350 settlers in a matter of hours.

I am now grown old, and must soon die; and the succession must descend, in order, to my brothers, Opitchapan, Opekankanough, and Catataugh, and then to my two sisters, and their two daughters. I wish their experience was equal to mine; and that your love to us might not be less than ours to you.

Why should you take by force that from us which you can have by love? Why should you destroy us, who have provided you with food? What can you get by war? We can hide our provisions, and fly into the woods; and then you must consequently famish by wronging your friends. What is the cause of your jealousy? You see us unarmed, and willing to supply your wants, if you will come in a friendly manner, and not with swords and guns, as to invade an enemy.

To seal their friendship with the Quaker colonists of Pennsylvania, the Delaware Indians presented them in 1682 with this wampum shell-bead belt, depicting an Indian and a white man (with hat) *holding hands.*

(PENNSYLVANIA HISTORICAL SOCIETY)

I am not so simple, as not to know it is better to eat good meat, lie well, and sleep quietly with my women and children; to laugh and be merry with the English; and, being their friend, to have copper, hatchets, and whatever else I want, than to fly from all, to lie cold in the woods, feed upon acorns, roots, and such trash, and to be so hunted, that I cannot rest, eat, or sleep. In such circumstances, my men must watch, and if a twig should but break, all would cry out, "Here comes Captain Smith"; and so, in this miserable manner, to end my miserable life; and, Captain Smith, this might be soon your fate too, through your rashness and unadvisedness.

I, therefore, exhort you to peaceable councils; and, above all, I insist that the guns and swords, the cause of all our jealousy and uneasiness, be removed and sent away.

WAHUNSONACOCK, *Powhatan Confederacy*

· 2 ·

Mary Jemison Becomes an Iroquois

A curiosity of the history of Native American and white relations are the "captivity narratives," firsthand accounts by whites who had been abducted by Indians. For three centuries this early American literary genre was relished by the general public, and the often lurid tales of torture and hardship generally reinforced the popular image of the Indian as a bloodthirsty savage. A few of these narratives, however, such as the story of the abduction in 1758 of Mary Jemison, age fifteen, by a Shawnee raiding party and her subsequent adoption by the Iroquois, tell of the captive's integration into Indian culture. For Indians, race was no barrier to this sort of reverse assimilation, as Mrs. Jemi-

son describes in this excerpt from her autobiography, published in 1824. She died at the age of ninety, an Iroquois grandmother on the Buffalo Creek Reservation in northern New York.

Having made fast to the shore, the squaws left me in the canoe while they went to their wigwam or house in the town, and returned with a suit of Indian clothing, all new, and very clean and nice. My clothes, though whole and good when I was taken, were now torn in pieces, so that I was almost naked. They first undressed me and threw my rags into the river; then washed me clean and dressed me in the new suit they had just brought, in complete Indian style; and then led me home and seated me in the center of their wigwam.

I had been in that situation but a few minutes, before all the squaws in the town came in to see me. I was soon surrounded by them, and they immediately set up a most dismal howling, crying bitterly, and wringing their hands in all the agonies of grief for a deceased relative.

Their tears flowed freely, and they exhibited all the signs of real mourning. At the commencement of this scene, one of their number began, in a voice somewhat between speaking and singing, to recite some words to the following purport, and continued the recitation till the ceremony was ended; the company at the same time varying the appearance of their countenances, gestures and tone of voice, so as to correspond with the sentiments expressed by their leader:

"Oh, our brother! Alas! He is dead—he has gone; he will never return! Friendless he died on the field of the slain, where his bones are yet lying unburied! Oh, who will not mourn his sad fate? No tears dropped around him; oh, no! No tears of his sisters were there! He fell in his prime, when his arm was most needed to keep us from danger! Alas! he has gone! and left us in sorrow, his loss to bewail: Oh, where is his spirit? . . . His spirit has seen our distress, and sent us a helper whom with pleasure we greet. Dickewamis has come: then let us receive her with joy! She is handsome and pleasant! Oh! she is our sister, and gladly we welcome her here. In the place of our brother she stands in our tribe. With care we will guard her from trouble; and may she be happy till her spirit shall leave us."

In the course of that ceremony, from mourning they became serene—joy sparkled in their countenances, and they seemed to rejoice over me as over a long-lost child. I was made welcome amongst them as a sister to the two squaws before mentioned, and was called Dickewamis; which being interpreted, signifies a pretty girl, a handsome girl, or a pleasant, good thing. That is the name by which I have ever since been called by the Indians.

I afterwards learned that the ceremony I at that time passed through, was that of adoption. The two squaws had lost a brother in Washington's war, sometime in the year before, and in consequence of his death went up to Fort Pitt, on the day on which I arrived there, in order to receive a prisoner or an enemy's scalp, to supply their loss. . . .

It was my happy lot to be accepted for adoption; and at the time of the ceremony I was received by the two squaws, to supply the place of their brother in the family; and I was ever considered and treated by them as a real sister, the same as though I had been born of their mother.

During my adoption, I sat motionless, nearly terrified to death at the appearance and actions of the company, expecting every moment to feel their vengeance, and suffer death on the spot. I was, however, happily disappointed, when at the close of the ceremony the company retired, and my sisters went about employing every means for my consolation and comfort.

Young Santiago McKinn, a white captive in a Chiricahua Apache camp.
(LOS ANGELES COUNTY MUSEUM OF NATURAL HISTORY)

Being now settled and provided with a home, I was employed in nursing the children, and doing light work about the house. Occasionally I was sent out with the Indian hunters, when they went but a short distance, to help them carry their game. My situation was easy; I had no particular hardships to endure. But still, the recollection of my parents, my brothers and sisters, my home, and my own captivity, destroyed my happiness, and made me constantly solitary, lonesome and gloomy.

My sisters would not allow me to speak English in their hearing; but remembering the charge that my dear mother gave me at the time I left her, whenever I chanced to be alone I made a business of repeating my prayer, catechism, or something I had learned in order that I might not forget my own language. By practising in that way I retained it till I came to Genesee flats, where I soon became acquainted with English people with whom I have been almost daily in the habit of conversing.

My sisters were diligent in teaching me their language; and to their great satisfaction I soon learned so that I could understand it readily, and speak it fluently. I was very fortunate in falling into their hands; for they were kind good natured women; peaceable and mild in their dispositions; temperate and decent in their habits, and very tender and gentle towards me. I have great reason to respect them, though they have been dead a great number of years.

The town where they lived was pleasantly situated on the Ohio, at the mouth of the Shenanjee: the land produced good corn; the woods furnished plenty of game, and the waters abounded with fish. Another river emptied itself into the Ohio, directly opposite the mouth of the Shenanjee. We spent the summer at that place, where we planted, hoed, and harvested a large crop of corn, of an excellent quality. . . .

The corn being harvested, the Indians took it on horses and in canoes, and proceeded down the Ohio, occasionally stopping to hunt a few days, till we arrived at the mouth of Sciota river; where they established their winter quarters, and continued hunting till the ensuing spring, in the adjacent wilderness. While at that place I went with the other children to assist the hunters to bring in their game. The forests on the Sciota were well stocked with elk, deer, and other large animals; and the marshes contained large numbers of beaver, muskrat, etc., which made excellent hunting for the Indians; who depended, for their meat, upon their success in taking elk and deer; and for ammunition and clothing, upon the beaver, muskrat, and other furs that they could take in addition to their peltry.

The season for hunting being passed, we all returned in the spring to the mouth of the river Shenanjee, to the houses and fields we had left in the fall before. There we again planted our corn, squashes, and beans, on the fields that we occupied the preceding summer.

About planting time, our Indians all went up to Fort Pitt, to make peace with the British, and took me with them. We landed on the opposite side of the river from the fort, and encamped for the night. Early the next morning the Indians took me over to the fort to see the white people that were there. It was then that my heart bounded to be liberated from the Indians and to be restored to my friends and my country. The white people were surprized to see me with the Indians, enduring the hardships of a savage life, at so early an age, and with so delicate a constitution as I appeared to possess. They asked me my name; where and when I was taken—and appeared very much interested on my behalf. They were continuing their inquiries, when my sisters became alarmed, believing that I should be taken from them, hurried me into their canoe and recrossed the river—took their bread out of the fire and fled with me, without stopping, till they arrived at the river Shenanjee. So great was their fear of losing me, or of my being given up in the treaty, that they never once stopped rowing till they got home.

Shortly after we left the shore opposite the fort, as I was informed by one of my Indian brothers, the white people came over to take me back; but after considerable inquiry, and having made diligent search to find where I was hid, they returned with heavy hearts. Although I had then been with the Indians something over a year, and had become considerably habituated to their mode of living, and attached to my sisters, the sight of white people who could speak English inspired me with an unspeakable anxiety to go home with them, and share in the blessings of civilization. My sudden departure and escape from them, seemed like a second captivity, and for a long time I brooded the thoughts of my miserable situation with almost as much sorrow and dejection as I had done those of my first sufferings. Time, the destroyer of every affection, wore away my unpleasant feelings, and I became as contented as before. . . .

Not long after the Delawares came to live with us [during the first summer], my sisters told me that I must go and live with one of them, whose name was Sheninjee. Not daring to cross them, or disobey their commands, with a great degree of reluctance I went; and Sheninjee and I were married according to Indian custom.

Sheninjee was a noble man; large in stature; elegant in his appearance; generous in his conduct; courageous in war; a friend to peace, and a great lover of justice. He supported a degree of dignity far above his rank, and merited and received the confidence and friendship of all the tribes with whom he was acquainted. Yet, Sheninjee was an Indian. The idea of spending my days with him, at first seemed perfectly irreconcilable to my feelings: but his good nature, generosity, tenderness, and friendship towards me, soon gained my affection; and, strange as it may seem, I loved him! To me he was ever kind in sickness, and always treated me with gentleness; in fact, he was an agreeable husband, and a comfortable companion. We lived happily together till the time of our final separation, which happened two or three years after our marriage, as I shall presently relate. . . .

MARY JEMISON, *Iroquois*

· 3 ·

Our Very Good Friend Kirk

President Thomas Jefferson had shrewdly assigned a Quaker to the Shawnee tribe when he implemented his plan for "civilizing" Indians by having them don European-style clothing, attend school, and most important, abandon hunting in favor of farming. The Quaker creed of nonviolence and interracial harmony had made the Pennsylvania Colony, founded in 1681 by William Penn, an oasis of neighborliness between white and Indian. In this selection, written in 1809, the Shawnee petition Jefferson to retain a Quaker named Kirk, possibly a government agent, of whom they were particularly fond. Their tribe had been dwelling in their western Ohio villages for only fourteen years when they sent this note. In another twenty years, they would be forced to sell that homesite and move west yet again.

It has been three years since we met together at the seat of Government you then told us that we ought to take care of our women and children and provide well for them we took your advice, at that time you told us you would send a man to help us and that man a Quaker went by us coming from you. You thought him a good man in appointing him.

Since that man has come to live with us, our women and children have found the benefit of it. they have had plenty to eat and he has helped us to make fences round our cornfields. Since he has been with us we have done well by his assistance to work with the young men that we find the benefit of it now, and you told us if we would cultivate the Land with him that we would become independent. we find this to be true. last summer we had plenty of corn and every kind of vegetables. our young men are always very glad to have our friend working with them. our friend is now about building a mill for us. We hope to find the benefit of it when it is done. our young men is glad to see it and we hope you will go through the work as it is begun and we will be independent in a short time our friend likes all our people and when they meet they are always glad to see each other. he always gives them good advice.

Since our friend Kirk has lived with us, we have always found him a good man. we are very fond of him. the white people in the State of Ohio are also fond of him. we do not want to part with him as he is a good man. we wish him to return and live with us. the white people all wish him to return. The Wyandotts are also very fond of him and have requested us to say that they wish him to return and take charge of our business again. We hope our Father [the President] will not listen to the bad stories that have gone about against our friend for they are all false. we therefore hope our Father will send him back to us.

Our hearts felt sorry when we found our friend was dismissed. all our people are fond of him and we are sorry to part with him. we hope our Father will not take him away from us but send him back again soon. we hope he will send an answer to this soon in order to make our minds easy, as our hearts will feel sorry until we hear of his coming back. this is all we have to say it is the sentiments of our hearts.

Signed,	THE OLD SNAKE his mark	X
"	THE WOLF his mark	X
"	CAPT. BUTLER his mark	X
"	THE BLACK HOOF his mark	X
"	YOUNG SNAKE his mark	X
"	THE BEAVER his mark	X
"	a Deleware Chief WAHAPPI	X

THE OLD SNAKE, ET AL., *Shawnee*

· 4 ·

The Frenchman
Dreams Himself Home

This Winnebago tale, concerned with intermarriage and half-white offspring, emphasizes the high value Native Americans place upon their children. The narrative, describing the reintegration into the tribe of a part-Winnebago, part-French boy, clearly shows that cultural allegiances were more important than racial purity. As happens with much oral tradition, more than one story has been interwoven here. The account of how these People of Real Speech, as the Winnebago called themselves, first met the French in the mid-seventeenth century has been grafted on to the story of the later arrival in Wisconsin of a Frenchman known to us only as Decora. The resulting legend of the founding of the Decora family lineage among the Winnebago was told to the anthropologist Paul Radin around 1910.

Once something appeared in the middle of the lake [Green Bay in Lake Michigan]. They were the French; they were the first to come to the Winnebago. The ship came nearer and the Winnebago went to the edge of the lake with offerings of tobacco and white deerskins. There they stood. When the French were about to come ashore, they fired their guns off in the air as a salute to the Indians. The Indians said, "They are thunderbirds." They had never heard the report of a gun before that time and that is why they thought they were thunderbirds.

Then the French landed their boats and came ashore and extended their hands to the Winnebago, and the Indians put tobacco in their hands. The French, of course, wanted to shake hands with the Indians. They did not know what tobacco was, and therefore did not know what to do with it. Some of the Winnebago poured tobacco on their heads, asking them for victory in war. The French tried to speak to them, but they could not, of course, make themselves understood. After a while they discovered that they were without tools, so they taught the Indians how to use an ax and chop a tree down. The Indians, however, were afraid of it, because they thought that the ax was holy. Then the French taught the Indians how to use guns, but they held aloof for a long time through fear, thinking that all these things were holy.

Suddenly a Frenchman saw an old man smoking and poured water on him. They knew nothing about smoking or tobacco. After a while they got more accustomed to one another. The Indians learned how to shoot the guns and began trading objects for axes. They would give furs and things of that nature for the guns, knives, and axes of the whites. They still considered them holy, however. Finally they learned how to handle guns quite well and they liked them very much. They would even build fires at night so that they might try their guns, for they could not wait for the day, they were so impatient. When they were out of ammunition, they would go to the traders and tell their people that they would soon return. By this time they had learned to make themselves understood by various signs.

The second time they went to visit the French, they took with them all the various articles that they possessed. There the French taught them how to sew, how to use an ax, and how to use a knife. Then the leader of the whites took a liking to a Winnebago girl, the daughter of the chief, and he asked her parents for permission to marry her. They told him that her two brothers had the right to give her away in marriage. So he asked them and they consented. Then he married her. He lived there and worked for the Indians and stayed with them for many years and he taught them the use of many tools. He went home every once in a while and his wife went with him, but he always came back again. After a while a son was born to him and then another. When the boys were somewhat grown up, he decided to take his oldest son with him to his country and bring him up in such a way that he would not be in danger, as was the case here in the woods. The Indians consented to it and they agreed that the mother was to bring up the youngest child.

So he took his oldest boy home with him, and when he got home, he went to live with his parents, as he had not been married in his own country. He was a leader of men. The boy was with him all the time and everyone took a great liking to him. People would come to see him and bring him presents. They gave him many toys. However, in spite of all, he got homesick and he would cry every night until he fell asleep. He cried all the time and would not eat. After a while the people thought it best to bring him back to his home, as they were afraid that he would get sick and die. Before long they brought him back. The father said: "My sons are men and they can remain here and grow up among you. You are to bring them up in your own way and they are to live just as you do."

The Indians made them fast. One morning the oldest one got up very early and did not go out fasting. His older uncle, seeing him try to eat some corn, took it away from him and, taking a piece of charcoal, mashed it, rubbed it over his face, and threw him out of doors. He went out into the wilderness and hid himself in a secret place. Afterwards the people searched for him everywhere, but they could not find him. Then the people told the uncle that he had done wrong in throwing the boy out. The latter was sorry, but there was nothing to be done anymore. In reality the uncle was afraid of the boy's father. They looked everywhere but could not find him.

After a full month the boy came home and brought with him a circle of wood (i.e., a drum). He told the people that this is what he had received in a dream, and that it was not to be used in war; that it was something with which to obtain life. He said that if a feast was made to it, this feast would be one to Earthmaker, as Earthmaker had blessed him and told him to put his life in the service of the Winnebago.

From this man they received many benefits. He was called to take the foremost part in everything. They called him the Frenchman, his younger brother being called *Tcaposgaga*, Whitethroat. And as they said, so it has always been. A person with French blood has always been the chief. Only they could accomplish anything among the whites. At the present time there is no clan as numerous as the descendants of that family and the object that he said was sacred (the drum) is indeed sacred. It is powerful to the present day. His descendants are the most intelligent of all the people and they are becoming more intelligent all the time. What they did was the best that could be done. The ways of the white man are best. That is the way they were brought up.

This is the end of the history of the Decoras.

ANONYMOUS, *Winnebago*

· 5 ·

Incident at Boyer Creek

This account of a run-in between Omaha Indian hunters and Mormon farmers in western Iowa dramatizes basic conflicts in Indian and white philosophies of life. Particularly it reveals how the issue of the land simmered just beneath the surface in nearly all Indian and white dealings. Differences in food-gathering habits and in concepts of ownership of property lie behind this story of a skirmish that never became a war. It was told in the 1880's by an unidentified Omaha to the anthropologist J. O. Dorsey. The incident took place in 1853.

We killed deer when we went on the autumnal hunt. We hunted all sorts of small leaping animals. When we approached any place to pitch the tents, we were in excellent spirits. Day after day we carried into camp different animals, such as deer, raccoons, badgers, skunks, and wild turkeys. We had ten lodges in our party. As we went, we camped for the night. And we camped again at night, being in excellent spirits.

At length we reached a place where some white farmers dwelt. They gave us food, which was very good. At length they assembled us. "Come, ye Indians, we must talk together. Let us talk to each other at night."

"Yes," said we.

As they came for us when a part of the night had passed, we said, "Let us go." They came with us to a very large house. Behold, all of the whites had arrived. That place was beyond the Little Sioux River, at Boyer Creek, where the first white men were, across the country from this place. They talked with us.

"Oho! my friends, though I, for my part, talk with you, you will do just what I say," said one.

"We will consider it. If it be good, we will do so," said the Omahas.

"I am unwilling for you to wander over this land," said the white man.

White Buffalo in the Distance said, "As you keep all your stock at home, you have no occasion to wander in search of them; and you dwell nowhere else but at this place. But we have wild animals, which are beyond our dwelling place, though they are on our land."

"Though you say so, the land is mine," said the white man.

"The land is not yours. The President did not buy it. You have jumped on it. You know that the President has not bought it, and I know it full well," said White Buffalo in the Distance.

"If the President bought it, are you so intelligent that you would know about it?" said the white man, speaking in a sneering manner to the Omaha.

White Buffalo in the Distance hit the white man several times on the chest. "Why do you consider me a fool? You are now dwelling a little beyond the bounds of the land belonging to the President. It is through me that you shall make yourself a person [i.e., you shall improve your condition at my expense]. I wish to eat my animals that grow of their own accord, so I walk seeking them," said White Buffalo in the Distance.

"Nevertheless, I am unwilling. If you go further, instead of obeying my words, we shall fight," said the white man.

"I will go beyond. You may fight me. As the land is mine, I shall go," said White Buffalo in the Distance.

"Yes, if you go tomorrow, I will go to you to see you. I shall collect the young white people all around, and go with them to see you," said the white man.

Having removed the camp in the morning, we scattered to hunt for game. I went with three men. About forty white men arrived, and stood there to intercept us. They waved their hands at us, saying, "Do not come any further." As we still went on, they came with a rush, and tried to snatch our guns from us. When we refused to let them go, they shot at us: "Ku! ku! ku!"

As we went back, we were driven towards the rest of our party. The leader of the white men said, "Do not go. If you go, I will shoot at you." We stood on an island; and the white men surrounded us.

"You have already shot at us," said the Omahas.

The white men doubted their word, saying, "It is not so about us."

"You have already shot at us, so we will go at all hazards. I am following my trail in my own land. I am going to hunt. Why do you behave so? Make way for us. We will go to you," said White Buffalo in the Distance.

"If you speak saucily to me, I will shoot at you," said the white man.

"Ho! if you wish to do that, do it," said the Omahas. As they departed, the whites made way for them.

We went along a bluff, and then downhill, when we reached a creek. It was a good place for us to stay, so we remained there.

At length about two hundred white men came in sight. We were just thirty. We were in the hollow by the edge of the stream. Wanacejiñga . . . arrived in sight. He looked at them. When he made a sudden signal, he was wounded in the arm. "They have wounded me! There is cause for anger! They have wounded me severely," said he.

"Oho! come, let us attack them at any rate," said the Omahas. We all stood, and gave the scalp yell. Having formed a line, we went to attack them. We scared off the white men. All of them were mounted; but only one Omaha, Agahamaci, was on a horse. He rode round and round, and gave us directions what to do. "Miss in firing at the white men. Shoot elsewhere every time," said he.

At length the Omahas intercepted the retreat of the whites. "Come, stop pursuing. Let us cease. It is good not to injure even one of the white people, who are our own flesh and blood," said Agahamaci. We returned to the women. Then we departed. We reached a place where we pitched the tents. There were a great many deer; they were exceedingly abundant.

ANONYMOUS, *Omaha*

· 6 ·
If I Could See This Thing

Native Americans lacked all resistance to what in the long run proved to be the most deadly aspect of living in company with whites—their diseases. The dread smallpox began killing Indians as early as 1514, when it first appeared in Panama. Successive epidemics of it continued throughout the nineteenth century. Disease was the overwhelming cause for the estimated 90 percent drop in Indian population between 1492 and 1900. No tribe was left unscathed, as smallpox, cholera, "the great red skin" (measles), tuberculosis, scarlet fever, and influenza took a greater toll than warfare or starvation.

Here George Bent, a part-white, part-Cheyenne trader, describes the terrible cholera scourge of 1849. Originating in the ports of New York and New Orleans, the disease was carried to the Great Plains by gold rushers, where it struck Bent's relatives.

In '49, the emigrants brought the cholera up the Platte Valley, and from the emigrant trains it spread to the Indian camps. "Cramps" the Indians called it, and they died of it by the hundreds. On the Platte whole camps could be seen deserted with the tepees full of dead bodies, men, women and children.

The Sioux and Cheyennes, who were nearest to the road [wagon train], were the hardest hit, and from the Sioux the epidemic spread northward clear to the Blackfeet, while from the Cheyennes and Arapahos it struck down into the Kiowa and Comanche country and created havoc among their camps.

Our tribe suffered very heavy loss; half of the tribe died, some old people say. A war party of about one hundred Cheyennes had been down the Platte, hunting for the Pawnees, and on their way home they stopped in an emigrant camp and saw white men dying of cholera in the wagons. When the Cheyennes saw these sick white men, they rushed out of the camp and started for home on the run, scattering as they went; but the terrible disease had them already in its grip, and many of the party died before reaching home, one of my Indian uncles and his wife dying among the first.

The men in the war party belonged to different camps, and when they joined these camps, they brought the cholera with them and it was soon raging in all the villages. The people were soon in a panic. The big camps broke up into little bands and family groups, and each little party fled from the rest.

When in 1856 smallpox struck the North Dakota Mandan for the fourth time, Running Face was five years old. He bore until his death the scars from the disease. (SMITHSONIAN INSTITUTION)

[My] grandmother (White Thunder's widow) and [my] stepmother, Yellow Woman, took the children that summer out among the Cheyennes, and they went to the Canadian, I think, where the Kiowas and Comanches were to make medicine. During the medicine dance an Osage visitor fell down in the crowd with cholera cramps. The Indians broke camp at once and fled in every direction, the Cheyennes north toward the Arkansas. They fled all night and halted on the Cimarron.

Here a brave man whose name I have forgotten—a famous warrior—mounted his war horse with his arms and rode through the camp shouting, "If I could see this thing [the cholera], if I knew where it was, I would go there and kill it!" He was taken with the cramps as he rode, slumped over on his horse, rode slowly back to his lodge, and fell to the ground. The people then broke camp in wild fright and fled north through the big sand hills all that night.

GEORGE BENT, *Southern Cheyenne*

· 7 ·

All Things Are Connected

Like the account of the incident at Boyer Creek, given earlier in the chapter, this 1855 letter from the Dwamish chief Seattle of Washington Territory to President Franklin Pierce reflects some of the contrasts in Indian and white attitudes toward the natural world.

We know that the white man does not understand our ways. One portion of the land is the same to him as the next, for he is a stranger who comes in the night and takes from the land whatever he needs. The earth is not his brother, but his enemy, and when he has conquered it, he moves on. He leaves his fathers' graves, and his children's birthright is forgotten. The sight of your cities pains the eyes of the red man. But perhaps it is because the red man is a savage and does not understand.

There is no quiet place in the white man's cities. No place to hear the leaves of spring or the rustle of insect's wings. But perhaps because I am a savage and do not understand, the clatter only seems to insult the ears. The Indian prefers the soft sound of the wind darting over the face of the pond, the smell of the wind itself cleansed by a mid-day rain, or scented with a piñon pine. The air is precious to the red man. For all things share the same breath—the beasts, the trees, the man. Like a man dying for many days, he is numb to the stench.

What is man without the beasts? If all the beasts were gone, men would die from great loneliness of spirit, for whatever happens to the beasts also happens to man. All things are connected. Whatever befalls the earth befalls the sons of the earth.

It matters little where we pass the rest of our days; they are not many. A few more hours, a few more winters, and none of the children of the great tribes that once lived on this earth, or that roamed in small bands in the woods, will be left to mourn the graves of a people once as powerful and hopeful as yours.

The whites, too, shall pass—perhaps sooner than other tribes. Continue to contaminate your bed, and you will one night suffocate in your own waste. When the buffalo are all slaughtered, the wild horses all tamed, the secret corners of the forest heavy with the scent of many men, and the view of the ripe hills blotted by talking wires, where is the thicket? Gone. Where is the eagle? Gone. And what is it to say goodby to the swift and the hunt, the end of living and the beginning of survival? We might understand if we knew what it was that the white man dreams,

The Dwamish chief, Seattle. (UNIVERSITY OF WASHINGTON)

what he describes to his children on the long winter nights, what visions he burns into their minds, so they will wish for tomorrow. But we are savages. The white man's dreams are hidden from us.

SEATTLE, *Dwamish*

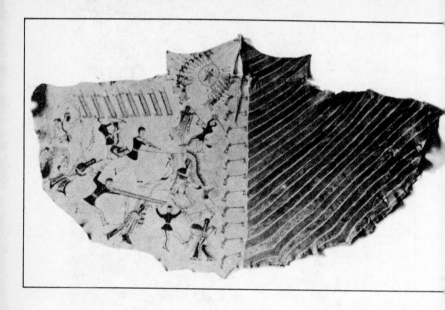

THE LONG
RESISTANCE

The Native American's homeland was not seized without a fight, many fights in fact. The four centuries of bitter warfare between red man and white took place in overlapping phases from the East Coast to the West between 1500 and 1900. The overriding cause was Native American resistance to white encroachment on tribal lands. The inevitable outcome—on the field of battle, at least—was Indian defeat.

The European powers were accustomed to waging grand military campaigns to resolve their territorial disputes. They had developed a professional-soldier caste and elaborate strategies for pitting trained armies against one another.

The Indian tribes, on the other hand, never kept standing armies. Their warriors were never exclusively professional soldiers in the European sense. Generally their raids were undertaken for reasons of personal revenge and not to build an empire or to exterminate their foes. With the coming of the horse to the Great Plains, intertribal feuding grew into almost a formalized sport.

The ordinary Indian man, although perfectly ready to defend

A battle between Kiowa warriors and United States troops, as depicted on a southern Plains tipi. (SMITHSONIAN INSTITUTION) his life or community, was at the same time a diligent family man, provider, craftsman, and participant in his people's demanding social and religious schedule. Even in the face of overwhelming threat to his existence, he strove to maintain the accustomed way of life. Thus, in 1814, the Creek warrior William Weatherford described the ideal conditions for defending his nation against the Georgia state militia: "I would have raised corn on one bank of the river and fought them on the other."

Combat between whites and Indians in North America falls into three major periods. The first saw the tribes resisting the rapacity of the Spanish, a sequence of hostilities that began shortly after the arrival of Columbus and lessened only after Spain reconquered the Pueblo Indians in New Mexico in 1692—although Spanish and Indian animosity would persist until Spain was finally forced to abandon her colonies in the 1820's. Overlapping this warfare in the Southwest was the incredibly complex period of incessant hostilities east of the Mississippi among the English, the French, and a multitude of Native American peoples, beginning with the Virginia uprising in 1622 and ending with the close of the War of 1812. Finally came the Indian efforts to hold off domination by the United States, starting with a series of wars in the 1790's and ending symbolically a century later with the tragic massacre at Wounded Knee in South Dakota.

The Spanish threw veteran soldiers of fortune and skilled cavalry against relatively peaceful, settled Indian communities in Florida, California, and the Southwest. These hardened campaigners shocked the Indians as they unhesitatingly enslaved or ruthlessly destroyed any native societies that stood between them and the gold and silver they sought.

During the Colonial era the British, French, and Spanish used the new continent as a battleground for their Old World rivalries. Wise Indian leaders sensed the danger of being swept into this power struggle. "Why do not you and the French fight in the old country and the sea?" the Delaware chief Shingas asked the British in 1758. "Why do you come to fight on our land? This makes everybody believe you want to take the land from us by force and settle it." (The British later considered Shingas such a threat that in 1775 their General Braddock offered a 200-pound bounty for Shingas's scalp, along with five pounds for the scalp of an ordinary warrior.)

Like many Indian headmen, Pontiac, an Ottawa chieftain from what is now the state of Michigan, became caught up in England and France's contest over New World supremacy. His dislike for the British stemmed from their trade policies—they had stopped dealing in rum and gunpowder with the Indians—and their mistreatment of the Allegheny mountain tribes. Although the French had lost the French and Indian War and been decisively defeated in Canada, Pontiac still hoped to revive their prominence.

Together with a Delaware Indian seer known as "the Enlightened," Pontiac formed the greatest alliance of fighting tribes since King Philip's confederacy of Indians had fought the New England colonists in 1675. The war he started in 1763 spread like wildfire across the Ohio Valley, but when his followers learned that France and England had secretly concluded a peace treaty, Pontiac's conspiracy collapsed. Although the Pontiac uprising caused the British government to issue a proclamation forbidding settlement in the Ottawa tribal lands, that restriction meant little to the American settlers who shortly flooded into the territory.

Most tribes found it impossible to maintain their neutrality; they were swayed by bribes, or they were bound by trade alliances, or they chose to exploit the strife to get revenge on old enemies. In the Southeast many Indian communities now found themselves caught between the British and the colonists. When the Mississippi Chickasaws were belatedly asked in 1782 to join the side of the American colonists in the Revolutionary War, they replied, "Our making a Peace with you doth Not Intitle Us to Fall out With Our Fathers the Inglish for we Love them as They were the First People that Ever Supported Us to Defend Our Selves Against Our former Enimys the French & Spaniards & All their Indians."

Other tribes, including the Shawnee, Mohawk, Seneca, and bands of the Delaware and Cherokee, sided with the Redcoats (the British) against the upstart Long Knives (the Americans). As a Delaware chief explained the alliance, "The father [England] has called on his Indian children, to assist him in punishing his children, the Americans. . . . At first I looked upon it as a family quarrel, in which I was not interested. However at length it appeared to me, that the father was in the right; and his children deserved to be punished a little. That this must be the case I concluded from the many cruel acts his offspring had committed from time to time on his Indian children. . . ."

During and after the Revolution, the United States took revenge against England's Indian allies. In August 1779, American troops launched a "scorched earth," campaign, burning to the ground forty Iroquois towns. Thereafter, among the Onondaga, Seneca, and Mohawk, George Washington was known as "the Town Destroyer." The tribes knew they were no longer warring to preserve political independence as had seemed to be the case in the 1760's. They were defending themselves against annihilation.

In 1789 the United States War Department was created, in part to handle all Indian matters. When a separate Bureau of Indian Affairs was established in 1824, it remained under War Department control. For the next quarter century, until the

Bureau of Indian Affairs was transferred to the Department of the Interior, the "Indian problem" was considered a military matter.

The United States wars with the Indians concentrated on three major fronts: (1) 1790–1832, the northeast wars, where American forces subjugated the remaining nations who had befriended the British; (2) 1849–1887, the southwestern campaigns across Arizona, New Mexico, and northern Mexico to vanquish the Navajo and Apache; (3) 1849–1892, the western Indian wars, a series of desperate clashes from Texas north to the Canadian border and westward to the Pacific Ocean.

In the seventeenth and eighteenth centuries, bows and arrows could hold their own against the smooth-bore muzzle-loaders used by the Europeans, though tribesmen eagerly sought to trade for these flintlocks whenever possible. But in the latter half of the nineteenth century, repeating rifles, constant replacements, and the contributions of Indian scouts would tip the balance in favor of the American soldiers. Often short of powder and shot for whatever firearms they had acquired by trade or theft, the Indians had but one real advantage: familiarity with the terrain. Whether darting through the Eastern Woodlands, wheeling on horseback across the Great Plains, or disappearing into the expanses of desert in the Southwest, hit-and-run Native American guerillas usually tried to avoid the costly, decisive battles so common to white warfare. In disbelief, Black Hawk, the Sauk chief, witnessed the British fighting during the War of 1812: "Instead of stealing upon each other, and taking every advantage to kill the enemy and save their own people . . . they march out, in open daylight, and fight, regardless of the number of warriors they may lose! After the battle is over, they retire to feast, and drink wine, as if nothing happened; after which, they make a statement in writing, of what they have done—each party claiming the victory!"

For centuries whites hired Indians to fight Indians. Here, a Warm Springs Indian scout, Loa-Kum-Artnuk, aims his Spencer rifle against Modoc hostiles during the famous 1872 war along the Oregon-California border.

(U.S. SIGNAL CORPS, NATIONAL ARCHIVES)

During the Revolution only a handful of Indians had served as American scouts, but in the western struggles with the Indians the United States Army took full advantage of old tribal animosities, recruiting scouts from among the Osage, Kansas, Crow, Arikara, Pawnee, and Apache. These "red bluecoats," often formed into special Indian scouting units, were invaluable in guiding cavalry columns, spotting the movements of hostile Indians, and later policing the new reservations.

In the long history of Indian-white warfare, the majority of Native American "uprisings" occurred when Indian territory was being encroached upon or some local incident ignited a frontier already tense with injustice toward the Indians. This was the case in 1675 when the execution of three Wampanoag tribesmen in Plymouth Colony touched off the long-smoldering anger of the New England tribes. Led by King Philip, himself a Wampanoag, the tribes waged a six-month campaign against white settlers, a war that represented the first major Indian effort to mount a multitribal offensive.

During later conflicts, actions by Indians were often exaggerated by settlers and sensationalized by frontier newsmen to justify a cry for troops that would smash the Indians once and for all. Within the Native American world, resentments against white injustices were frequently given focus by an accompanying native religious revival. Indian leaders often had a prophet-seer at their side, who prophesied a restoration of Indian traditional life once the whites were driven into the sea, or once the Indians learned to reject white ways and vices.

On the military scoreboard the Indians enjoyed a few short-lived successes, including Opechancanough's 1622 rout of the Jamestown settlers; the 1680 crushing of Spanish rule in the Southwest by the united Pueblo tribes; Little Turtle's thrashing of General Arthur St. Clair's American troops in the Ohio Valley in 1791; Little Crow's surprise attacks on Minnesota pioneers in 1862; the victory of Red Cloud in 1868, when the use of the Bozeman Trail, which ran through Indian-held territory guaranteed by treaty, had to be abandoned; and the annihilation of General George A. Custer's command in 1876. But the Native American was never able to follow up on such successes; his strategy was always short-range. Even his most charismatic leaders could not keep a multitribal military force together for long. And neither stealthy ambushes nor full-scale assaults could stem the unending stream of white reinforcements. In the end the Indian was simply outnumbered as well as outarmed. Warfare against the whites was at best only a holding action. Native fighting prowess was judged finally by how long a tribe could prolong its retreat or delay its surrender.

The accounts that follow represent but a handful of the countless campaigns, massacres, and skirmishes that took place and add up to the longest war in American history.

· 1 ·
We Must Be United

After the colonies were free from England's domination a remarkable Shawnee leader began rallying many of the same Indians who had fought beside Pontiac. His name was Cougar Crouching for His Prey, or Tecumseh, and he had earned his warrior's reputation fighting in the defeats of General Harmer at Fort Wayne (1790) and General St. Clair on the Wabash River (1791). Now the enemy were the Americans who had settled along the Monongahela, Allegheny, and Ohio rivers. Like Pontiac, too, Tecumseh's movement was furthered by a holy man, his brother, who was called "The Prophet." Tecumseh envisioned a vast coalition of tribes who would fight to recover the Ohio Valley lands lost through a succession of dubious treaties negotiated by the wily American governor of Indiana Territory, William H. Harrison.

In 1810–11, Tecumseh traveled from the Great Lakes to the Gulf of Mexico, trying to elicit support for his cause. In the selection that follows, he is speaking to the Osage. Before returning from this pilgrimage, however, American troops found Tecumseh's stronghold, known as Prophet's Town, on the Tippecanoe River and burned it to the ground. The great leader's gathering storm never broke. Tecumseh died in Canada on October 5, 1813, fighting on the British side against his old adversary Willian H. Harrison in the Battle of the Thames.

Brothers—We all belong to one family; we are all children of the Great Spirit; we walk in the same path; slake our thirst at the same spring; and now affairs of the greatest concern lead us to smoke the pipe around the same council fire!

Brothers—We are friends; we must assist each other to bear our burdens. The blood of many of our fathers and brothers has run like water on the ground, to satisfy the avarice of the white men. We, ourselves, are threatened with a great evil; nothing will pacify them but the destruction of all the red men.

Brothers—When the white men first set foot on our grounds, they were hungry; they had no place on which to spread their blankets, or to kindle their fires. They were feeble; they could do nothing for themselves. Our fathers commiserated their distress, and shared freely with them whatever the Great Spirit had given his red children. They gave them food when hungry, medicine when sick, spread skins for them to sleep on, and gave them grounds, that they might hunt and raise corn.

Brothers—The white people are like poisonous serpents: when chilled, they are feeble, and harmless, but invigorate them with warmth, and they sting their benefactors to death.

The white people came among us feeble; and now we have made them strong, they wish to kill us, or drive us back, as they would wolves and panthers.

Brothers—The white men are not friends to the Indians: at first, they only asked for land sufficient for a wigwam; now, nothing will satisfy them but the whole of our hunting grounds, from the rising to the setting sun.

Brothers—The white men want more than our hunting grounds; they wish to kill our warriors; they would even kill our old men, women, and little ones.

Brothers—Many winters ago, there was no land; the sun did

not rise and set: all was darkness. The Great Spirit made all things. He gave the white people a home beyond the great waters. He supplied these grounds with game, and gave them to his red children; and he gave them strength and courage to defend them.

Brothers—My people wish for peace; the red men all wish for peace; but where the white people are, there is no peace for them, except it be on the bosom of our mother.

Brothers—The white men despise and cheat the Indians; they abuse and insult them; they do not think the red men sufficiently good to live.

The red men have borne many and great injuries; they ought to suffer them no longer. My people will not; they are determined on vengeance; they have taken up the tomahawk; they will make it fat with blood; they will drink the blood of the white people.

Brothers—My people are brave and numerous; but the white people are too strong for them alone. I wish you to take up the tomahawk with them. If we all unite, we will cause the rivers to stain the great waters with their blood.

Brothers—If you do not unite with us, they will first destroy us, and then you will fall an easy prey to them. They have destroyed many nations of red men because they were not united, because they were not friends to each other.

Brothers—The white people send runners amongst us; they wish to make us enemies, that they may sweep over and desolate our hunting grounds, like devastating winds, or rushing waters.

Brothers—Our Great Father over the great waters [the king of England] is angry with the white people, our enemies. He will send his brave warriors against them; he will send us rifles, and whatever else we want—he is our friend, and we are his children.

Brothers—Who are the white people that we should fear them? They cannot run fast, and are good marks to shoot at: they are only men; our fathers have killed many of them; we are not squaws, and we will stain the earth red with their blood.

Brothers—The Great Spirit is angry with our enemies; he speaks in thunder, and the earth swallows up villages, and drinks up the Mississippi. The great waters will cover their lowlands; their corn cannot grow; and the Great Spirit will sweep those who escape to the hills from the earth with his terrible breath.

Brothers—We must be united; we must smoke the same pipe; we must fight each other's battles; and more than all, we must love the Great Spirit; he is for us; he will destroy our enemies, and make his red children happy.

TECUMSEH, *Shawnee*

· 2 ·

Black Hawk Stands Alone

The next celebrated defender of Native American independence was the Sauk chief named Big Black Bird Hawk who had joined Tecumseh and fought with the British in 1812. This version of the series of skirmishes that became known as the Black Hawk War was related by tribal elders around 1910 to the part-Fox anthropologist, William Jones. It does not identify the treaty that set Black Hawk against the Americans. In 1804 Governor William Henry Harrison had prevailed upon three Sauk and Fox chiefs to sell, without tribal approval, all their northwestern Illinois lands; Harrison is believed to have gotten the Indians drunk first.

After Black Hawk and his people were finally expelled from their Rock Island wigwams in 1831, the chief crossed the Mississippi and returned to his Illinois homeland the following spring with a thousand followers. Immediately hounded by the Illinois militia, Black Hawk successfully fought them off, but he had a harder time with federal troops and Indian mercenaries under the command of General Henry Atkinson. The Battle of Bad Axe along the Mississippi River, where more than two hundred of his people were killed—men, women, and children— effectively ended Black Hawk's four months of rebellion.

The Sauks and Foxes were living together at the time, in the Rock River country. White people had been coming in for some time, and helping themselves to the land. Wherever they selected places to live, there they settled down and began to make homes for themselves. The people beheld these doings, and were not at all pleased. When they made protests, the reply they got was that the land was no longer theirs, that it was now the white man's.

About this time came officers of the government, and the chiefs and head men met them in council. The white men presented a paper. It said that an agreement had been made between officers of the government and head men of the Sauks and Foxes; that according to the agreement, the people had given up the possession of all the Rock River country, in return for which the government had paid money, sugar, coffee, pork, tobacco, salt, and whiskey; and at the bottom of the paper was signed the names of the men of both sides who made the agreement. The principal man on the side of the government was the head official at Shallow Water (St. Louis); and the principal man on the side of the Sauks and Foxes was Kwaskwami. The agreement had been made in the wintertime.

The whole business came with great surprise upon the chiefs and councillors. The paper made clear one thing: it verified the ugly rumors that had gone from mouth to mouth about Kwaskwami. It was known to all that he had gone to spend the winter near Shallow Water. His object was to be near a trading post where he could dispose of his pelts as fast as he got them. But it was rumored that he spent much time at the post, and that he hunted little; that he hobnobbed with the big official there, and that he had much money to spend; that he drank a great deal, and was often so drunk that he was absent from his camp for a long period at a time; and that all the while, even up to the time of his departure, he had plenty of food to eat.

Now, all this was very strange, and the people wondered how it had come to pass. Then, as now, they knew they kept tab on the wealth of one another, and it was easy to guess the limit of one's possessions. Moreover, it was particularly easy to guess how much a man like Kwaskwami had. . . . Kwaskwami and the men whose names were on the paper denied ever having touched the pen. They must have lied, or else they were drunk at the time and did not know they had touched the pen.

The chiefs and councillors tried to explain to the officers the position of Kwaskwami—that the man was not a chief; that he had no power to make a treaty with another nation; that his act was not known before or at the time he did it; that he was not made a delegate to make a treaty on behalf of his people; and that what he did, he did as an individual. They tried to explain to the officers that it was necessary, when a question came up about the cession of land, to let the whole nation know about it; and that when a cession was made, it was necessary first to get the consent of every chief and councillor.

It was of no use to talk about these things. The officers said that the agreement had been made, and that both parties would have to stand by it; that they had come, not to talk about the treaty, but to tell the people to move as soon as possible across to the west bank of the Mississippi.

Naturally the people were loath to leave their old homes; but some had made up their minds to make the best of a bad bargain, and go to the new country. Those most of this mind were the Foxes. Pawicig was chief of the Foxes then, and he led his people over across the river. With the Foxes went a band of Sauks.

Among the Sauks was a man who had been prominent in council; his name was Keokuk.

Most of the Sauks were not for going, especially men of the younger class. There was at this time among the Sauks a great warrior; he was of the Thunder Clan, and his name Big Black Bird Hawk. The young men rallied about him, and talked to him about holding the old home, even if it meant war with the white man. He was not willing at first, because the number of his Sauk warriors was not big enough for a long, hard fight; and they had few guns and little ammunition, though they all had bows and arrows. He had fought with the English and with the Shawnee Tecumseh, and knew what it was to fight against the government.

In the midst of these events, he was visited by emissaries from other nations—from the Potawatomies, Kickapoos, Winnebagoes, Omahas, and the Sioux—all of them offering help to drive back the white man. A prophet among the Potawatomies told of a vision he had of the manitou [sacred spirit] by which power came to him to foretell events. He said that the Big Black Bird Hawk was the man to lead the nations and win back the old homes of the people; that when the fight began, speedily would rise the dead to life again, and the warriors would be without number; that back would come the buffalo and the game-folk that had disappeared; and that in a little while the white man would be driven to the eastern ocean and across to the farther shore from whence he came.

In the end the Big Black Bird Hawk was prevailed upon to go to war. No sooner had he begun, when he discovered that he would have to do the fighting with only the warriors of his own nation and a few others that came from the Kickapoos and Foxes. The chief of the Potawatomies who had urged him so strongly to fight gave the alarm to the white people, and took sides with them as soon as the fighting began. Instead of the Sioux and Omahas coming to his help, they fought against him; and when the Winnebagoes saw how things were going, they joined also with the whites. Indeed, there was little fighting between the Sauks and the white men; most of the fighting was between the Sauks and the other nations. It was the Winnebagoes who made the Big Black Bird Hawk captive. They turned him over to the white men, who carried him away to the east and kept him there a prisoner. After a time he was permitted to return to his people, whom he found living on the west bank of the Mississippi. A short while after he died. Some white men stole his skeleton, and placed it in a great building, where it was on view. The great building caught fire; and it was burned up with the bones of the warrior of the Thunder Clan.

WILLIAM JONES, *Fox*

· 3 ·

Blood Scattered like Water

The Bloody Island Massacre of 1850 took place during the darkest period of California Indian history. Anti-Indian sentiment was at a fever pitch: between 1848 and 1870 some fifty

*thousand Native Americans—contemptuously termed Diggers
—died, killed by the military, by citizen-organized "Indian
hunts," and by disease. Between 1850 and 1863 an estimated ten
thousand California Indians—children preferred—were sold or
indentured for cheap labor in the United States and Mexico.*

*Among such outrages was the murder of over a hundred Pomo
Indian men, women, and children on an island in Pomo County's
Clear Lake—"a perfect slaughter pen" in the words of the
United States army officer whose troops did the deed.*

*Here Chief William Benson, born twelve years after the event,
gives his people's version of what happened. It opens with the
murder of Stone and Kelsey, two former trappers, who had
abused a band of starving, semi-enslaved Pomos. Attempting
to rustle cattle to stay alive, the Indians accidentally lose
their overseers' horse. Realizing they will be punished, they
decide to kill Stone and Kelsey, their bosses. Although they flee,
it is with a foreboding sense of the terrible punishment that
awaits them.*

The Facts of Stone and Kelsey Massacre, in Lake County,
California, as it was stated to me by the five Indians who went
to Stone and Kelsey's house [with the] purpose to kill the two
white men. After debating all night.

Shuk and Xasis. These two men were the instigators of the
massacre. . . . Shuk and Xasis was foremans for the herds [of
Stone and Kelsey]. And only those herds got anything to eat.
Each one of these herders got four cups of wheat for a day's
work. This cup would hold about one and a half pints of water.
The wheat was boiled before it was given to the herders. And
the herders shire [shared it] with their families. The herders
who had large families were also starving. About twenty old

people died during the winter from starvation. From severe whipping, four died. A nephew of an Indian lady who was living with Stone was shoot to death by Stone. . . . [the Indians suffered] whipping and tieing their hands together with rope. The rope [was] then thrown over a limb of a tree and then drawn up until the Indian's toes barly touch[ed] the ground and let them hang there for hours. This was common punishment. When a father or mother of young girl was asked to bring the girl to his house by Stone or Kelsey, if this order was not obeyed, he or her would be whipped or hung by the hands. Such punishment occurred two or three times a week. And many of the old men and women died from fear and starvation. . . .

The starvation of the Indians was the cause of the massacre of Stone and Kelsey. The Indians who were starving hired a man by the name of Shuk and another man by the name of Xasis. To kill a beef for them. . . .

Shuk got a chance and threw the rope on the large ox. Xasis came as quick as he could, [but] the band then began to stampede. The ox also started with the band. The ground was wet and slippery, and [it was] raining. And before Xasis could get his rope on, Shuk's horse fell to the ground. The horse and the ox got away. Xasis tried to lasso the horse but could not get near it to throw the rope. . . . The two went back to the camp and reported to the people who hired them. Told them the bad luck they had. . . .

All the men who [had] hired Shuk and Xasis had gathered in Xasis' house. Here they debated all night. Shuk and Xasis wanted to kill Stone and Kelsey. They said Stone and Kelsey would kill them as soon as they would find out that the horses was taken without them known; one man got up and suggested that the tribe give Stone and Kelsey forty sticks of beads which means 16,000 beads, or 100 dollars. No one agreed. Another man suggested that he or Shuk, tell Stone or Kelsey that the horse was stolen. No one agreed. And another man suggested that the other horse should be turned out, and [they should] tell Stone and Kelsey [that] both horses were stolen. No one agreed. . . .

While this debating was going on the hired or servant boys and girls of Stone's and Kelsey's were told by Shuk and Xasis to carry out all the guns. Bows and arrows, knives and everything like weapons were taken out of the house by these girls and boys, so the two white men were helpless in defense. . . .

So the five men went to the house where Stone and Kelsey were living, at daylight in the place where Stone always built a fire under a large pot in which he boiled wheat for the Indian herders, about 16 of them. These five men waited around this pot until Stone came out to build the fire. Stone came out with a pot full of fire which was taken from the fireplace. And said to the Indians: "What's the matter, boys? You came early this morning. Some thing wrong?" The Indians said: "Oh, nothing. Me hungry, that's all."

Qka-Nas—or Cayote Jim as he was known by the whites— Qka-Nas said to the men: "I thought you men came to kill this man; give me these arrows and bow." He jerk[ed] the bow and the arrows away from Shuk and drew it, and as he did, Stone rose quickly and turned to Qka-Nas and said, "What are you trying to do, Jim?" And as Stone said it, the Indian cut loose. The arrow struck the victim [in the] pit of the stomach. The victim immediately pulled the arrow out and ran for the house. Fighting his way, he broke one man's arm with the pot he had. And succeeded in getting in the house and locked the door after him.

A little later Kelsey came and opened the door and noticed the blood on the doorstep. The Indians advanced. Kelsey saw that the Indians meant business. He said to them: *"No matar* [Don't kill] Kelsey. Kelsey *bueno hombore para vosotros* [a good man for you]." The Indians charged and two of the Indians caught Kelsey and the fight began. In this fight Kelsey was stabbed twice in the back. . . .

And then they called all the people to come and take what wheat and corn they could pack and go to a hiding place, where they could not be found by the whites. So the Indians of both villages came and took all the wheat and corn they could gather in the place, and then went to hide themselves. Some went to Fishel's Point and some went to Scotts Valley. The men went out to kill cattle for their use, and every man who was able to ride caught himself a horse. In around the valley and upper lake and Bachelor Valley, there were about one thousand head of horses and about four thousand head of cattles. So the Indians lived fat for a while. . . .

Two or three weeks had passed. No white men were seen on either trail. One day Qka-Nas and Ma-Laq-Que-Tou saw two white men on horseback come over the hill. They stopped on top of the hill. They saw nothing staring around Stone and Kelsey's place. No Indians in the village. Qka-Nas and Ma-Laq-Que-Tou went around behind a small hill to cut the white men off. The white men saw the Indians trying to go around behind them. The whites turned and went back before the Indians got in back of them. So three or four days went by. No more white man was seen. . . .

For three days they watch[ed] the lake. One morning they saw a long boat came up the lake with [a] pole on the bow with [a] red cloth. And several of them came. Every one of the boats had ten to fifteen men. The smoke signal was given by the two watchmen. Every Indian around the lake knew the soldiers were coming up the lake. And how many of them. And those who were watching the trail saw the infantry coming over the hill from [the] lower lake. These two men were watching from Ash Hill. They went to Stone and Kelsey's house. From there the horsemen went down torge [toward] the lake and the soldiers went across the valley torge Lakeport. They went on to Scotts Valley. Shoot a few shoots with their big gun and went on to Upper Lake and camped on Emerson Hill. From there they saw the Indian camp on the island. The next morning the white warriors went across in their long dugouts. The Indians said they would meet them in peace. So when the whites landed, the Indians went to welcome them but the white man was determined to kill them.

Ge-Wi-Lih said he threw up his hands and said, "No harm, me good man." But the white man fired and shot him in the arm, and another shot came and hit a man standing along side of him and was killed. So they had to run and fight back; as they ran back in the tuleys [bulrushes] and hid under the water; four or five of them gave a little battle and another man was shot in the shoulder. Some of them jumped in the water and hid in the tuleys. Many women and children were killed on [or] around this island.

One old lady, a Indian told about what she saw while hiding under a bank in under a cover of hanging tuleys. She said she saw two white men coming with their guns up in the air and on their guns hung a little girl. They brought it to the creek and threw it in the water. And a little later two more men came in the same manner. This time they had a little boy on the end of their guns and also threw it in the water. A little ways from her she said lay a woman shot through the shoulder. She held her little baby in her arms. Two white men came running torge [toward] the woman and baby. They stabbed the woman and the baby and threw both of them over the bank in to the water. She said she heard the woman say, "O my baby"; she said when they gathered the dead, they found all the little ones were killed by being stabbed, and many of the women were also killed [by] stabbing. She said it took them four or five days to gather up the dead: And the dead were all burnt on the east side of the creek. . . .

The next morning the soldiers started for Mendocino County. And there killed many Indians. The camp was on the ranch now known as Ed Howell ranch. The soldiers made camp a little ways below about one half mile from the Indian camp. The Indians wanted to surrender. But the soldiers did not give them time. The soldiers went in the camp and shot them down as if they were dogs. Some of them escaped by going down a little creek leading to the river. And some of them hid in the brush. And those who hid in the brush most of them were killed. And those who hid in the water was overlooked. They killed mostly women and children. . . .

One old man told me about the soldiers killing the Indians in this same camp. He must have been about 18 or 20 years of age. He said he and another boy about the same age was taken by the soldiers and he said there were two soldiers in charge of them. One would walk ahead and one behind them. . . . They both were barefooted, he said, when they began to climb the mountain between Mendocino and Lake County. He said they were made to keep up with the soldiers. When they were climbing over the Bottlerock Mountain, their feet were cut up by the rocks and their feet were bleeding and they could not walk up with the soldiers. The man behind would jab them with the sharp knife fixed on the end of the gun. . . .

Two or three days later the chief soldier told them they could go back. They was then given meat and bread. All they could pack. He said they started back on their journey. He said it was all most difficult for them to walk but [they] wrapped a lot of cloth around their feet and by doing so made their way all right. . . .

Now and then they would side track, and look back to see if the soldiers were following them. After seeing no soldiers following them, they would start out for another run. He said they traveled in such manner until they got to their home. He said to himself: Here I am not to see my mother and sister but to see their blood scattered over the ground like water and their bodies for coyotes to devour. He said he sat down under a tree and cryed all day.

WILLIAM BENSON, *Pomo*

· 4 ·
Young Men,
Go Out and Fight Them

The gold rush of 1874, which lured thousands of white prospectors into the Black Hills of South Dakota, was a crucial factor in provoking a major confrontation between the United States and the Plains Indians. To the powerful Sioux nation these mountains were sacred terrain, and also properly protected by the Laramie Treaty of 1868, signed by the Sioux and the United States government. It was Lieutenant Colonel George Armstrong Custer who originally violated that treaty. In July 1874, ostensibly to locate a site for a new fort, but covertly to hunt for mineral resources, Custer led the expedition into the Black Hills and reported that there was gold "from the grassroots down."

So it was poetic justice that in late June 1876 Custer's small command should blunder into the largest gathering of Plains Indian fighters ever assembled—an estimated twelve to fifteen thousand Indians, with at least four thousand fighting men, drawn from the Teton, Santee and Yankton Sioux, Assiniboine, Cheyenne, Arapaho, and Gros Ventre, camped together along three miles of the bank of the Little Big Horn River in central Montana. Under the leadership of the Sioux war chiefs Sitting Bull and Crazy Horse and the Cheyenne headman Two Moons, the natives were comprised of die-hard hostiles and recent reservation runaways come together haphazardly to present a united, confident front.

Here is one warrior's memory of the tumultuous day of "many soldiers falling into camp," the battle of the Little Big Horn. Wooden Leg, the narrator, was about eighteen years old when Custer disastrously divided his Seventh Cavalry forces, ignored warnings from his Crow scouts, and was cut down along with all 225 of his officers and men. The battle was a freakish victory for the Indians, stunning the victors along with the vanquished. The tribes did not have sufficient unity or ammunition to follow it up with a broader offensive. Their forces quickly scattered, with Sitting Bull and his followers hiding out in Canada until 1881.

In my sleep I dreamed that a great crowd of people were making lots of noise. Something in the noise startled me. I found myself wide awake, sitting up and listening. My brother too awakened, and we both jumped to our feet. A great commotion was going on among the camps. We heard shooting. We hurried out from the trees so we might see as well as hear.

Wooden Leg.

The shooting was somewhere at the upper part of the camp circles. It looked as if all of the Indians there were running away toward the hills to the westward or down toward the village. Women were screaming and men were letting out war cries. Through it all we could hear old men calling: "Soldiers are here! Young men, go out and fight them."

We ran to our camp and to our home lodge. Everybody there was excited. Women were hurriedly making up little packs for flight. Some were going off northward or across the river without any packs. Children were hunting for their mothers. Mothers were anxiously trying to find their children. I got my lariat and my six-shooter. I hastened on down toward where had been our horse herd. . . .

My father had caught my favorite horse from the herd brought in by the boys and Bald Eagle. I quickly emptied out my war bag and set myself at getting ready to go into battle. I jerked off my ordinary clothing. I jerked on a pair of new breeches that had been given to me by an Uncpapa Sioux. I had a good cloth shirt, and I put it on. My old moccasins were kicked off and a pair of beaded moccasins substituted for them.

My father strapped a blanket upon my horse and arranged the rawhide lariat into a bridle. He stood holding my mount. "Hurry," he urged me.

The air was so full of dust I could not see where to go. But it was not needful that I see that far. I kept my horse headed in the direction of movement by the crowd of Indians on horseback. I was led out around and far beyond the Uncpapa camp circle. Many hundreds of Indians on horseback were dashing to and fro in front of a body of soldiers. The soldiers were on the level valley ground and were shooting with rifles. Not many bullets were being sent back at them, but thousands of arrows were falling among them. I went on with a throng of Sioux until we got beyond and behind the white men. By this time, though, they had mounted their horses and were hiding themselves in the timber. . . .

Suddenly the hidden soldiers came tearing out on horseback, from the woods. I was around on that side where they came out. I whirled my horse and lashed it into a dash to escape from them. All others of my companions did the same. But soon we discovered they were not following us. They were running away from us. They were going as fast as their tired horses could carry them across an open valley space and toward the river. We stopped, looked a moment, and then we whipped our ponies into swift pursuit. A great throng of Sioux also were coming after them. A distant position put them among the leaders in the chase. The soldier horses moved slowly, as if they were very tired. Ours were lively. We gained rapidly on them.

I fired four shots with my six-shooter. I do not know whether or not any of my bullets did harm. I saw a Sioux put an arrow into the back of a soldier's head. Another arrow went into his shoulder. He tumbled from his horse to the ground. Others fell dead either from arrows or from stabbings or jabbings or from blows by the stone war clubs of the Sioux. Horses limped or staggered or sprawled out dead or dying.

Our war cries and war songs were mingled with many jeering calls, such as: "You are only boys. You ought not to be fighting. We whipped you on the Rosebud. You should have brought more Crows or Shoshones with you to do your fighting."

Little Bird and I were after one certain soldier. Little Bird was wearing a trailing warbonnet. He was at the right and I was at the left of the fleeing man. We were lashing him and his horse with our pony whips. It seemed not brave to shoot him. Besides, I did not want to waste my bullets. He pointed back his revolver, though, and sent a bullet into Little Bird's thigh.

Immediately I whacked the white man fighter on his head with the heavy elk-horn handle of my pony whip. The blow dazed him. I seized the rifle strapped on his back. I wrenched it and dragged the looping strap over his head. As I was getting possession of this weapon, he fell to the ground. I did not harm him further. I do not know what became of him. The jam of oncoming Indians swept me on. . . .

I returned to the west side of the river. Lots of Indians were hunting around there for dead soldiers or for wounded ones to kill. I joined in this search. I got some tobacco from the pockets of one dead man. I got also a belt having in it a few cartridges. All of the weapons and clothing and all other possessions were being taken from the bodies. The warriors were doing this. No old people nor women were there. They all had run away to the hill benches to the westward.

I went to a dead horse, to see what might be found there. Leather bags were on them, behind the saddles. I rummaged into one of these bags. I found there two pasteboard boxes. I broke open one of them. "Oh, cartridges!"

There were twenty of them in each box, forty in all. Thirty of them were used to fill up the vacant places in my belt. The remaining ten I wrapped into a piece of cloth and dropped them down into my own little kit bag. Now I need not be so careful in expending ammunition. Now I felt very brave. . . .

The shots quit coming from the soldiers. Warriors who had crept close to them began to call out that all of the white men were dead. All of the Indians then jumped up and rushed forward. All of the boys and old men on their horses came tearing into the crowd. The air was full of dust and smoke. Everybody was greatly excited. It looked like thousands of dogs might look if all of them were mixed together in a fight. All of the Indians were saying these soldiers also went crazy and killed themselves.

I do not know. I could not see them. But I believe they did so. . . .

I took one scalp. As I went walking and leading my horse among the dead, I observed one face that interested me. The dead man had a long beard growing from both sides of his face and extending several inches below the chin. He had also a full mustache. All of the beard hair was of a light yellow color, as I now recall it. Most of the soldiers had beards growing, in dif-ferent lengths, but this was the longest one I saw among them. I think the dead man may have been thirty or more years old. "Here is a new kind of scalp," I said to a companion. I skinned one side of the face and half of the chin, so as to keep the long beard yet on the part removed. I got an arrow shaft and tied the strange scalp to the end of it. . . .

I waved my scalp as I rode among our people. The first per-son I met took special interest in me was my mother's mother. She was living in a little willow dome lodge of her own. "What is that?" she asked me when I flourished the scalp stick toward her. I told her. "I give it to you," I said, and I held it out to her. She screamed and shrank away. "Take it," I urged. "It will be good medicine for you." Then I went on to tell her about my having killed the Crow or Shoshone at the first fight up the river, about my getting the two guns, about my knocking in the head two soldiers in the river, about what I had done in the next fight on the hill where all of the soldiers had been killed. We talked about my soldier clothing. She said I looked good dressed that way. I had thought so too, but neither the coat nor the breeches fit me well. The arms and legs were too short for me. Finally she decided she would take the scalp. She went then into her own little lodge. . . .

There was no dancing nor celebrating of any kind in any of the camps that night. Too many people were in mourning, among all of the Sioux as well as among the Cheyennes. Too many Cheyenne and Sioux women had gashed their arms and legs, in token of their grief. The people generally were praying, not cheering. There was much noise and confusion, but this was from other causes. Young men were going out to fight the first soldiers now hiding themselves on the hill across the river from where had been the first fighting during the morning. . . .

I did not go back that afternoon nor that night to help in fighting the first soldiers. Late in the night, though, I went as a scout. Five young men of the Cheyennes were appointed to guard our camp while other people slept. These were Big Nose, Yellow Horse, Little Shield, Horse Road and Wooden Leg. One or other of us was out somewhere looking over the country all the time. Two of us went once over to the place where the soldiers were hidden. We got upon hill points higher than they were. We could look down among them. We could have shot among them, but we did not do this. We just saw that they yet were there.

Five other young men took our duties in the last part of the night. I was glad to be relieved. I did not go to my family group for rest. I let loose my horse and dropped myself down upon a thick pad of grassy sod.

WOODEN LEG, *Northern Cheyenne*

· 5 ·

Geronimo Puts Down the Gun

Geronimo, whose Native American name, Goyathlay, means "One Who Yawns," was a Chiricahua Apache. In 1858 he returned to his home in southeastern Arizona to discover the dead bodies of his mother, wife, and three children; they had been killed by Mexican troops. From then on, Geronimo took every opportunity to terrorize Mexican settlements. As a warrior during the so-called Cochise wars of the 1860's, he fought against American soldiers. In the 1870's Geronimo was in charge as his Chiricahua band fled from the distasteful San Carlos reservation in southwestern Arizona to the wild, free backlands of Chihuaha and Sonora in Mexico and began marauding against Mexicans and Americans alike.

Frequently taken prisoner, Geronimo kept escaping until a major search by General George Crook led to his capture in 1883 in the Sierra Madre Mountains of Mexico. For two years Geronimo seemed to be settling into a quiet life of growing vegetables on the San Carlos Apache reservation. Then came the burst to freedom that is related here by Jason Betzinez, Geronimo's cousin, who was twenty-five years old at the time.

Geronimo's final surrender in 1887, described by Betzinez, put an end to significant Indian guerilla action in the United States. The weary fighter and over three hundred of his fellow Chiricahuas were shipped under heavy guard to Fort Marion, Florida. Among the prisoners of war were Apaches like Betzinez, who had never joined Geronimo, and even Apache scouts who had taken sides against him.

After settling on the Fort Apache reservation [San Carlos], Geronimo and many others made a beginning in the effort to change from warriors to farmers. Nevertheless turbulent days still lay ahead. . . .

In the spring of 1885 Geronimo, Chichuahua, Mangas (son of the old chief Mangas Colorado), and a number of others got to making and drinking Indian beer in violation of orders from the authorities. This homebrew made the Indians drunk and quarrelsome. They were brought before Lieutenant Davis who threatened to report them to General Crook. At this the Indians got the idea that they might be sent off to prison [to Alcatraz]. . . . Having been placed in irons once before, when the band was shipped to San Carlos, some of the leaders determined not to undergo such treatment again. They plotted to leave the reservation, taking their immediate families as well as some other Apaches whom they induced to go with them. . . .

As told you, I learned of all this as I was coming home from planting the barley field which Geronimo and I had been farming together. My brother-in-law having met me on the road, we discussed the whole situation. It appeared to us that we would have to go with our family group leader, Geronimo. Some of the young men who were our close friends and blood relatives had already joined him that very afternoon. Late that night I started off southward accompanied by my mother and sister. Then I told them to go on ahead, I wanted to return for my brother-in-law, who had not come with us. We would catch up with them later.

Unable to find my brother-in-law, I hastened to overtake my own family. As I hurried along the main road through the dark moonless night, my thoughts were very troubled. I came to the conclusion that it would be foolish to throw away what I was just beginning to learn of a better way of life. So when I came up with my mother and sister I informed them of this decision and told them to return to our camp. . . .

According to what we learned later, [those who left the reservation] crossed the Black River, climbed the mountains to the south, and camped on the summit where they could observe any pursuit. After resting there the remainder of the night they took off straight south toward the border, not stopping to camp again until they had covered 120 miles. After reaching Mexico they separated into several small groups each under its own chief. . . .

Two troops of the Fourth Cavalry together with some Indian scouts under Lieutenants Gatewood and Davis promptly followed but were unable to catch the runaways. People who have been in this rugged country can well understand how easily the Apaches, with their superior speed and endurance, and their willingness to take to the rocks and the mountain tops, were able to evade their pursuers.

Geronimo (front row, third from the right) *and other Chiricahua Apaches in 1886, outside a prison train bound for Florida.*

(U.S. SIGNAL CORPS, NATIONAL ARCHIVES)

Another habit of the Apaches contributed largely to their success in keeping out of reach. . . . It was a mysterious manner of vanishing completely when the soldiers and scouts had just caught up with them or were about to attack their camp. Each day the chief designated an assembly point. . . . Then when the troops would find them or were about to launch an attack the Indians would scatter, keeping their minds firmly fixed on the assembly point far away. The scouts, who were experienced warriors themselves, had a hard time tracking down the hostiles, as they were forced to follow the many diverging trails, most of which disappeared in the rocks anyway.

The hostiles would converge on their predetermined rendezvous point but instead of camping there would make an imitation camp. They would build several small campfires and tie an old worn-out horse to a tree to make it look as though the camp was occupied. Then they would move on for several miles and establish their real camp elsewhere. The scouts knowing that their fellow tribesmen, the hostiles, would assemble at nightfall, would lie in wait all through the night ready to attack at daybreak. The attack would land upon a fake camp. The scouts were of course disgusted and disappointed but presently they would laugh, saying, "Oh, my! We were fooled!" They took it as a great joke on themselves. . . .

General Miles came to Fort Apache in the summer of 1886 to plan a campaign for running down the Apaches who still remained out. He held a meeting at the agency at which I was present. He explained that he wanted to form a large expedition to corral Geronimo's band and thus bring all the Apache troubles to an end. Though most of the Indians present were Chiricahuas and Warm Springs Apaches, many of them related to Geronimo and his men, great enthusiasm was shown. The Indians were excited and happy over the prospect of going out on another campaign. Hardship and danger meant nothing, adventure was what they wanted and it didn't seem to matter that they were going to fight their own people. . . .

Meantime Geronimo and his warriors were moving slowly toward the U.S. border. It was August 1886. They had not been suffering but were driving some stolen cattle.

One day the scouts told Captain Lawton it would be a good idea to camp along the creek while Lieutenant Gatewood, Mr. George Wratten, Kayitah and Martine [Apache scouts], and ten soldiers should go out to find the hostiles. From the tracks and signs of old camps Kayitah thought that Geronimo was in the mountains to the east of this camp.

So this small party moved toward a long peak which the Apaches called Mountain Tall. At one point the ridge rose in a steep bluff. The keen eyes of the two Indians spotted something on top of the escarpment. Soon they realized that it was Geronimo's band. Motioning to Lieutenant Gatewood to stop his advance, the two Apaches moved up to the foot of the bluff. Kayitah shouted in a loud but quavering voice, "I am Kayitah. Let me come up. I have a message for you."

Geronimo called down, "All right. Come on. We'll listen."

Leaving the other men behind, the two scouts climbed up the steep mountain. Arriving at the summit, on legs trembling with fear, they saw Geronimo and his men there with ready guns. Up to that moment Kayitah and Martine didn't know whether they would be permitted to live. But the outlaws greeted them warmly. They really were glad to see each other, as close associates among the Apaches always were after a considerable separation. After much friendly chatter and a recounting of what had occurred since Geronimo had left, Kayitah delivered General Miles' message. The General wanted them to give themselves up without any guarantees.

For a few moments there was silence. The Indians seemed stunned. Finally Geronimo's half-brother White Horse [Leon Perico] spoke out. "I am going to surrender. My wife and children have been captured. I love them, and want to be with them."

Then another brother said that if White Horse was going, he would go too. In a moment the third and youngest brother made a similar statement.

Geronimo stood for a few moments without speaking. At length he said slowly, "I don't know what to do. I have been depending heavily on you three men. You have been great fighters in battle. If you are going to surrender, there is no use my going without you. I will give up with you."

JASON BETZINEZ, *Southern Chiricahua Apache*

THE
TREATY TRAIL

Although the drama of Indian-white warfare has always captured the popular imagination, Native Americans lost far more of their land and independence by the bloodless process of signing treaties than they ever did on the battlefield. Indeed, most of the violence between Indians and whites flared up because Native Americans were being deprived of the very land promised them in earlier treaties. "You give us presents, and then take our land," complained the Cheyenne spokesman Buffalo Chief at the famous Treaty of Medicine Lodge in 1867. "That produces war."

To the Indians the practice of drafting a written agreement to settle political and territorial disputes was alien and unfamiliar, and as a result, it was used against them to great advantage. As Red Cloud, the Oglala Sioux leader, recalled, "In 1868 men came out and brought papers. We could not read them, and they did not tell us truly what was in them. . . . When I reached Washington the Great Father explained to me what the treaty was, and showed me that the interpreters had deceived me."

In a rare photo, a Prairie Indian leader negotiates with white officials. Two of his fellow tribesmen (seated) *display medallions probably given to them during earlier diplomatic conferences.* (DENVER PUBLIC LIBRARY)

At first the European powers drew up treaties to cement relations with influential tribes, to "bury the tomahawk"—to use the famous phrase found in an early southern Plains treaty—with hostile Indians, and to formalize trading partnerships. During the period of New World colonization, the warring European nations used treaties to bolster their forces with Indian auxiliaries. As the white population grew, however, and Indian power waned, the documents became thinly disguised bills of sale, transferring ancient tribal lands into white hands.

In the fine print, these treaties usually called for Indians to move to the least fertile corner of their existing lands, to abandon their homes altogether and move elsewhere, or to slice up their holdings into single-family allotments, which the Indians were supposed to cultivate while selling off the rest to white land speculators. In some cases, whites reserved the right to run their wagon trails or railroad tracks across Indian land. Inevitably this brought trouble as settlers homesteaded and prospectors mined in country they were supposed to be only passing through.

The legal basis for making treaties with the Indians was established as early as the sixteenth century by lawyers for the Spanish court. Although vast portions of the New World were claimed by the conquistadors, Spain still felt that the Indians enjoyed some vague "aboriginal title" to the country. Ideally the king's envoys were to obtain the "voluntary consent" of Native Americans before usurping their lands. Other European and American legalists also granted Indians a "right of occupancy." Behind these manipulative phrases and contradictory postures lay the white man's vacillation between greed and conscience. He was determined to take possession of the territories he "discovered," but he needed to feel he was acquiring them fairly and legally. The muddled, controversial saga of Indian land loss shows the white man alternately behaving as the fair-minded negotiator trying to strike an honest bargain for the lands he had to have, and then as the ruthless land grabber employing any pseudo-legal scheme and threat of military power to drive the Native American from his home. By the mid-eighteenth century, treaty making was standard operating procedure for getting what one wanted from the Indians.

The young United States government negotiated its first Indian treaty during the Revolutionary War, wringing from the Delawares a 1778 pledge to help in the resistance to the British. (In return the Delawares were promised statehood, should they some time in the future desire it. This, of course, never materialized. Instead, over the next century the Delawares signed a series of eighteen treaties that would leave them entirely powerless and dispersed from Canada to Texas.)

In the Northwest Ordinance of 1787, in which Congress set forth principles for governing its landholdings west of the Appalachian Mountains, the United States promised that "utmost good faith shall always be observed towards the Indians; their land and property shall never be taken from them without their consent." But after 1800, treaties were contracted more in haste than good faith. Between 1800 and 1812, for instance, William Henry Harrison, superintendent of the Northwest Indians and governor of Indiana Territory, negotiated and speedily signed fifteen treaties with tribes who thereby yielded all of present-day Indiana, Illinois, a sizable chunk of Ohio, and portions of Michigan and Wisconsin—at the price of about a penny an acre. Farther west, between 1853 and 1857, Congress ratified fifty-two treaties by which tribes living in Idaho, Oregon, and Washington lost 157 million acres.

By this time, treaty making had degenerated into a hollow formality for inexpensively obtaining what would otherwise have required a military expedition to seize, and for conveniently removing Indians to backwater reservations, where once confined, they could be schooled in the ways of white American civilization. The last of the 374 treaties with Native Americans was signed in 1868, forcing Chief Joseph and his Nez Percé followers to move from their beloved Wallowa Valley in Oregon because gold had been discovered there. It also precipitated the short-lived Nez Percé War.

On March 3, 1871, Congress formally ended what Andrew Jackson had dismissed as "the farce of treating with Indian tribes." In passing that year's Indian Appropriation Act, Congress tacked on the stipulation that from then on, "No Indian nation or tribe within the territory of the United States shall be acknowledged and recognized as an independent nation, tribe, or power with whom the United States may contract by treaty." At the same time Congress took pains to reiterate the government's responsibility to honor all "lawfully made" treaties already in force. This decision was backed both by reformers, who denounced the corruption that had riddled such negotiations, and by anti-Indian politicians, who wanted to bury any suggestion that the tribes were sovereign nations. Thereafter the United States government made "agreements" and passed laws—about five thousand by 1940—for dealing with Indians.

Over the centuries Native American attitudes toward treaties changed from bewilderment to indignation to outrage. By the time Indians had grown aware of the opportunities for deception behind the bloodless exercise of treaty signing, it was usually too late. Lamented Black Hawk, the Sauk chieftain, "I touched the goose quill to the treaty, not knowing, however, that, by that act, I consented to give away my village."

A pervasive form of abuse throughout the centuries was to rush tribesmen into affixing their X marks or name pictographs to treaty agreements before they had had time to discuss the matter, either among themselves or in formal council. Often those who approved the treaty were any agreeable Indians the negotiators could hastily collect for a meeting, or a clan leader who was unauthorized to speak for the entire tribe. (One American emissary was overheard to brag that he would bring a treaty with the Sioux to a successful conclusion even if only two warriors signed.)

Government officials also exploited schisms within Indian communities, playing one side against the other. They often neglected to explain that presents lavished upon their Native American guests during treaty negotiations were actually partial payment for lands soon to be gone forever. They transformed treaty sessions into colorful, multitribal affairs, inviting those Indians who participated to make speeches, sport their brilliant costumes, and accept specially minted medallions before signing away their homelands. The Native American talent for instant recollection of the wording of ancient treaties sometimes, however, stymied white negotiators who wished to reinterpret their content. A common complaint among Indians was that government officials failed to make clear at the outset all the ramifications of the treaties they were signing. In the end, tribe after tribe was cajoled and threatened into renegotiating old agreements that had outlived their usefulness. In this respect the Potawatomi and Chippewa set the record; at the end of the treaty-making era, both tribes had signed forty-two successive treaties, each of them supposedly ironclad.

The durability of the promises contained in these treaties continues to be an explosive issue between Native Americans and the United States government today. Most of the documents included "in perpetuity" clauses, guaranteeing forever government outlays of food and clothing, aid and protection.

More critically, the treaties were transacted on the premise that both parties were equal, sovereign nations. The government wants to avoid debating that premise and instead clear up all outstanding treaty disputes through its Indian Claims Commission and by means of cash settlements. A growing number of Native American nationalists are, however, highly critical of cash payoffs. And they want to preserve the unique, political relationship that distinguishes their tribal communities from other ethnic groups. They want to resurrect the political premise of the old treaties and demand that vows of aid and protection be observed, in the words of an old trade agreement, "For as long as the grass shall grow and the rivers run."

The following accounts show Native Americans struggling to preserve their rights within the alien context of the white man's diplomatic game and its strange rules.

· 1 ·

Let Us Examine the Facts

Corn Tassel, an elderly Cherokee statesman, delivered this stinging reply to the United States commissioners who had come to sign a peace treaty with his tribe. The time was July 1785. The Cherokee had become well versed in the intricacies of power politics through their long dealings with France and England. They had actively sided with the British at the outbreak of the Revolutionary War, and as Corn Tassel makes clear they still felt themselves the equal of the Americans on the battlefield. The first part of this talk is a rebuttal to any claims to Cherokee land on the basis of right of conquest. Corn Tassel ends his remarks by insisting, as Indian orators frequently did, that whites must simply accept the irreconcilable differences between the two ways of life, and cease trying to transform Indians into white people.

It is a little surprising that when we entered into treaties with our brothers, the whites, their whole cry is *more land!* Indeed, formerly it seemed to be a matter of formality with them to demand what they knew we durst not refuse. But on the principles of fairness, of which we have received assurances during the conducting of the present treaty, and in the name of free will and equality, I must reject your demand.

Suppose, in considering the nature of your claim (and in justice to my nation I shall and will do it freely), I were to ask one of you, my brother warriors, under what kind of authority, by what law, or on what pretense he makes this exorbitant demand of nearly all the lands we hold between your settlements and our towns, as the cement and consideration of our peace.

Would he tell me that it is by right of conquest? No! If he did, I should retort on him that *we* had last marched over his territory; even up to this very place which he has *fortified* so far within his former limits; nay, that some of our young warriors (whom we have not yet had an opportunity to recall or give notice to, of the general treaty) are still in the woods, and continue to keep his people in fear, and that it was but till lately that these identical walls were your strongholds, out of which you durst scarcely advance.

If, therefore, a bare march, or reconnoitering a country is sufficient reason to ground a claim to it, we shall insist upon transposing the demand, and your relinquishing your settlements on the western waters and removing one hundred miles back towards the east, whither some of our warriors advanced against you in the course of last year's campaign.

Let us examine the facts of your present eruption into our country, and we shall discover your pretentions on that ground. What did you do? You marched into our territories with a superior force; our vigilance gave us no timely notice of your manouvres; your numbers far exceeded us, and we fled to the stronghold of our extensive woods, there to secure our women and children.

Thus, you marched into our towns; they were left to your mercy; you killed a few scattered and defenseless individuals, spread fire and desolation wherever you pleased, and returned again to your own habitations. If you meant this, indeed, as a conquest you omitted the most essential point; you should have fortified the junction of the Holstein and Tennessee rivers, and have thereby conquered all the waters above you. But, as all are fair advantages during the existence of a state of war, it is now too late for us to suffer for your mishap of generalship!

Again, were we to inquire by what law or authority you set up a claim, I answer, *none!* Your laws extend not into our country, nor ever did. You talk of the law of nature and the law of nations, and they are both against you.

Indeed, much has been advanced on the want of what you term civilization among the Indians; and many proposals have been made to us to adopt your laws, your religion, your manners and your customs. But, we confess that we do not yet see the propriety, or practicability of such a reformation, and should be better pleased with beholding the good effect of these doctrines in your own practices than with hearing you talk about them, or reading your papers to us upon such subjects.

You say: Why do not the Indians till the ground and live as we do? May we not, with equal propriety, ask, Why the white people do not hunt and live as we do? You profess to think it no injustice to warn us not to kill our deer and other game from the mere love of waste; but it is very criminal in our young men if they chance to kill a cow or a hog for their sustenance when they happen to be in your lands. We wish, however, to be at peace with you, and to do as we would be done by. We do not quarrel with you for killing an occasional buffalo, bear or deer on our lands when you need one to eat; but you go much farther; your people hunt to gain a livelihood by it; they kill all our game; our young men resent the injury, and it is followed by blood-shed and war.

This is not a mere affected injury; it is a grievance which we equitably complain of and it demands a permanent redress.

The great God of Nature has placed us in different situations. It is true that he has endowed you with many superior advantages; but he has not created us to be your slaves. *We are a separate people!* He has given each their lands, under distinct considerations and circumstances; he has stocked yours with cows, ours with buffalo; yours with hog, ours with bear; yours with sheep, ours with deer. He has, indeed, given you an advantage in this, that your cattle are tame and domestic while ours are wild and demand not only a larger space for range, but art to hunt and kill them; they are, nevertheless, as much our property as other animals are yours, and ought not to be taken away without our consent, or for something equivalent.

CORN TASSEL, *Cherokee*

· 2 ·

Osceola Determined

This is an edited transcript of a three-day meeting that took place in October 1823 between Seminole chieftains and General Wiley Thompson. Under dispute in the talks were two earlier treaties: the 1823 agreement at Camp Moultrie, Florida, signed by only a single faction of the tribe, under which the Seminole agreed to live on a reservation of four million acres, receiving annual payments of food and money in exchange; and the 1832 treaty at Payne's Landing, Florida, where again only a portion of the Seminole agreed to the treaty, requiring them to move to territory west of the Mississippi.

At the time of this meeting, Seminole leaders had already been taken to look over their prospective new home adjoining Creek Indian lands in Oklahoma. Thus the scene was set for the kind of classic confrontation—experienced by tribe after tribe—between Indian holdouts and impatient white officials anxious to have their way. Where the chiefs appear to be wavering, it was often because they were attempting to discover the consensus in their own group as it took shape before their eyes, and because, even in their beleaguered position, they shied away from showing open hostility toward a visitor. Notice the subtle role played by Osceola, at that time a young subchief, as he adamantly opposes removal, then sits back to let the words of his elders fly until, at the end, he decisively reenters the discussion.

A year after this clash of words, General Thompson was shot from ambush by a war party led by Osceola, and that same afternoon Jumper, Miconopy, and Alligator attacked two military companies, leaving only three soldiers barely alive. This marked the beginning of the Second Seminole War which lasted well after its recorded closing date of 1842, resulted in the deaths of fifteen hundred American troops, and cost the government twenty million dollars. Osceola was tricked into capture when he agreed to meet a group of soldiers under a flag of truce. Three months later, he died in prison. Many of the Seminoles eventually did remove, but several maverick bands clung to their stronghold in the Everglades where their descendants remain to this day.

Seminole Agency, Florida Territory
October 23, 1834, 11:00 A.M.

GENERAL THOMPSON: Friends and Brothers: I come from your great father, the President of the United States, with a talk: listen to what I say.

On the 9th of May, 1832, you entered into a treaty at Payne's Landing. I come from the President to tell you that he has complied with all his promises to you in that treaty that he was bound to do before you move, and that you must prepare to move by the time the cold weather of winter shall have passed away. . . .

The proposition which I present for your decision is:

1st. Will you accept the invitation of your brothers of the western Creek nation?

2nd. Do you prefer cattle or money, when you arrive at your new home, for the cattle, which, under the treaty, you must give up here?

3rd. Will you petition to go by water, or do you prefer to go by land?

4th. How will you have your next annuity paid to you, in money or in goods?

[*At this point one of the Seminole delegates, Holata Amaltha, announced that his group wanted to talk in private first, and would reconvene with Thompson the next morning. But Thompson must have planted a spy, for the talks that afternoon were "reported confidentially" and the following remains part of the official record.*]

OSCEOLA: My Brothers! The white people got some of our chiefs to sign a paper to give our lands to them, but our chiefs

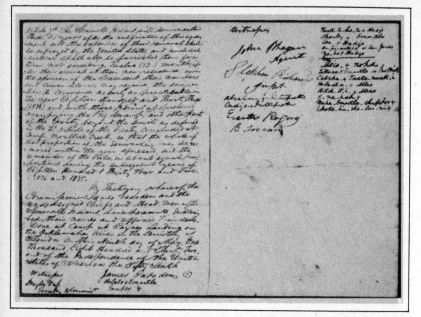

The signature pages of the 1832 treaty at Payne's Landing.

did not do as we told them to do; they done wrong; we must do right. The agent tells us we must go away from the lands we live on—our homes, and the graves of our Fathers, and go over the big river [the Mississippi] among the bad Indians. When the agent tells me to go from my home, I hate him, because I love my home, and will not go from it.

My Brothers! When the Great Spirit tells me to go with the white man, I go: but he tells me not to go. The white man says I shall go, and he will send people to make me go; but I have a rifle, and I have some powder and some lead. I say, we must not leave our homes and lands. If any of our people want to go west, we won't let them; and I tell them they are our enemies, and we will treat them so, for the Great Spirit will protect us.

HOLATA AMALTHA: My Brothers and Friends! You want to

hear my talk. When we made a treaty at Payne's, some of us said if the land was good for us, we would go across the great Mississippi. We were told, it would be better for the red people and the red people would be happy there; that if we stayed here the bad white men would wrong us; so we went to see the land our great father said we must have, and it was good land. We told the agents, whom our father sent with us, that we would do as our father bade us. My Brothers! I don't want to talk like a foolish child. My talk is good for my people; and I say we must act honest and do as our great father at Washington tells us.

JUMPER, "THE SENSE-KEEPER": My Brothers! You have listened to the talk of our brothers; now hear mine. I do not make talks today to break them tomorrow. I told the agent I was glad to see the lands which our great father said we must have, and I told him that I and my people would go, and we have no excuse. If we don't go, our father will send his men to make us go, and we will lose many of our tribe. . . .

October 24, 1834, 11:00 A.M.

[General Thompson asks the Seminoles for their reply]

HOLATA MICO: God made all of us, and we all came from one woman, sucked one bubby; we hope we shall not quarrel; that we will talk until we get through.

MICONOPY: When we were at Camp Moultrie we made a treaty, and we were to be paid our annuity for twenty years. That is all I have got to say.

JUMPER: At Camp Moultrie they told us all difficulties should be buried for twenty years, from the date of the treaty made there; that after this we held a treaty at Payne's Landing, before the twenty years were out; and they told us we might go and see the country, but that we were not obliged to remove.

The land is very good; I saw it, and was glad to see it; the neighbors there are bad people; I do not like them bad Indians, the Pawnees . . . the Indians there steal horses, and take packs on their horses; they all steal horses from the different tribes; I do not want to go among such people; your talk seems always good, but we don't feel disposed to go west.

HOLATA AMALTHA: The horses that were stolen from us by the Cherokees we never got back [*the horses had been stolen from the Seminoles while they were looking over their proposed new land*]. We then told the agent that the people were bad there. . . .

CHARLEY AMALTHA: My family I love dearly and sacredly. I do not think it right to take them off. . . . Should I go west, I should lose many on the path. As to the country west, I looked at it; a weak man cannot get there, the fatigue would be so great; it requires a strong man. I hardly got there. . . .

GENERAL THOMPSON: My talk to you yesterday must and will stand, and you must abide by it. . . . And I want, when you meet me again in council, that you give a correct account of the number of your people, that the government may provide for you comfortably while on your journey, whether by land or by water. . . . When you come here again, come prepared to act like chiefs, and honourable men; don't bring to me any more foolish talks. Men do not listen to the talks of a child; and remember that the talk I gave you must and will stand.

October 25, 1834, 11:00 A.M.

GENERAL THOMPSON: I am ready to receive your answers to the questions I submitted to you.

HOLATA MICO: I have only to repeat what I said yesterday,

and to say that twenty years from the Moultrie treaty has not yet expired. I never gave my consent to go west; the whites may say so, but I never gave my consent.

JUMPER: We are not satisfied to go until the end of the twenty years, according to the treaty at Camp Moultrie. We were called upon to go to the west, beyond the Mississippi. It is a good country; this is a poor country, we know. We had a good deal of trouble to get there; what would it be for all our tribe?

MICONOPY: I say, what I said yesterday, I did not sign the treaty.

GENERAL THOMPSON: Abraham [the interpreter], tell Miconopy that I say he lies; he did sign the treaty.

CHARLEY AMALTHA: The agent told us yesterday we did not talk to the point. I have nothing to say different. . . . At Payne's Landing the white people forced us into the treaty. I was there. I agreed to go west and did go west. I went in a vessel, and it made me sick. I undertook to go there; and think that, for so many people, it would have been very bad. . . .

GENERAL THOMPSON: The Creeks, Choctaws, Chickasaws, and Cherokees, who live in the states, are moving west of the Mississippi River, because they cannot live under the white people's laws. . . . Suppose, what is however impossible, that you could be permitted to remain here a few years longer, what would be your condition? This land will soon be surveyed, sold to, and settled by the whites. . . . Thus, you may see, that were it possible for you to remain here a few years longer, you would be reduced to hopeless poverty, and when urged by hunger to ask, perhaps, of the man who thus would have ruined you (and is perhaps now tampering with you for the purpose of getting your property) for a crust of bread, you might be called an Indian dog, and be ordered to clear out.

[*Osceola, seated beside Miconopy, urges the chief to be firm against removal.*]

GENERAL THOMPSON: Your father, the President, sees all these evils, and will save you from them by removing you west; and I stand up for the last time to tell you, that you must go; and if not willingly, you will be compelled to go. I should have told you that no more annuity will be paid to you here.

[*Osceola interrupts, saying he does not care whether any more money is paid his people.*]

GENERAL THOMPSON: I hope you will, on more mature reflection, act like honest men, and not compel me to report you to your father, the President, as faithless to your engagements.

[*Osceola says that the decision of the chiefs has been given; they will make no other answer.*]

MICONOPY: I do not intend to remove.

GENERAL THOMPSON: I am now fully satisfied that you are wilfully disposed to be entirely dishonest in regard to your engagements with the President, and regret that I must so report you. . . .

OSCEOLA, ET AL., *Seminole*

· 3 ·

My Son, Stop Your Ears

On January 14, 1879, a remarkable Indian was given a rare opportunity. Chief Joseph, the great Nez Percé leader, journeyed to Washington, D.C., to tell a full house of Congress why his people had gone on the warpath two years earlier.

He began his speech with a description of his forebears' amicable meeting with the explorers Lewis and Clark. In the excerpted selection presented below, he focuses on the treaties that the United States government signed with his tribe. Joseph's own band boycotted the signing of the most critical of these treaties —that of 1863, in which the tribal lands in the Wallowa area were supposedly ceded and which Joseph highlights here. Each year he and his loyal followers refused to leave their Oregon homes, and each year agents tried to remove them. In 1887 Joseph was about to relent when local cowboys stole several hundred Nez Percé horses. The Indians' pent-up anger exploded. During the next four months Joseph conducted an amazing guerrilla campaign, outwitting the pursuing troops led by General O. O. Howard over a distance of thirteen hundred miles, punctuated by desperate hand-to-hand skirmishes. The chase culminated in Chief Joseph's surrender almost within reach of freedom in Canada.

The Congressional speech fell on deaf ears. Joseph was held prisoner in Kansas for a while; five of his children perished of disease there. He never again saw his homeland and died in 1904 on the Coleville Reservation in the state of Washington.

It has always been the pride of the Nez Percés that they were the friends of the white men. When my father was a young man there came to our country a white man [Reverend Mr. Spaulding] who talked spirit law. He won the affections of our people because he spoke good things to them. At first he did not say anything about white men wanting to settle on our lands. Nothing was said about that until about twenty winters ago, when a number of white people came into our country and built houses and made farms. At first our people made no complaint. They thought there was room enough for all to live in peace, and they were learning many things from the white men that seemed to be good. But we soon found that the white men were growing rich very fast, and were greedy to possess everything the Indian had. My father was the first to see through the schemes of the white men, and he warned his tribe to be careful about trading with them. He had suspicion of men who seemed so anxious to make money. I was a boy then, but I remember well my father's caution. He had sharper eyes than the rest of our people.

Next there came a white officer [Governor Stevens], who invited all the Nez Percés to a treaty council. After the council was opened he made known his heart. He said there were a great many white people in the country, and many more would come; that he wanted the land marked out so that the Indians and white men could be separated. If they were to live in peace it was necessary, he said, that the Indians should have a country set apart for them, and in that country they must stay. My father, who represented his band, refused to have anything to do with the council, because he wished to be a free man. He claimed that no man owned any part of the earth, and a man could not sell what he did not own.

Mr. Spaulding took hold of my father's arm and said, "Come and sign the treaty." My father pushed him away, and said: "Why do you ask me to sign away my country? It is your business to talk to us about spirit matters, and not to talk to us about parting with our land." Governor Stevens urged my father to sign his treaty, but he refused. "I will not sign your paper," he said; "you go where you please, so do I; you are not a child, I am no child; I can think for myself. No man can think for me. I have no other home than this. I will not give it up to any man. My people would have no home. Take away your paper. I will not touch it with my hand."

My father left the council. Some of the chiefs of the other bands of the Nez Percés signed the treaty, and then Governor Stevens gave them presents of blankets. My father cautioned his people to take no presents, for "after a while," he said, "they will claim that you have accepted pay for your country." Since that time four bands of the Nez Percés have received annuities from the United States. My father was invited to many councils, and they tried hard to make him sign the treaty, but he was firm as the rock, and would not sign away his home. His refusal caused a difference among the Nez Percés.

Eight years later (1863) was the next treaty council. A chief called Lawyer, because he was a great talker, took the lead in this council, and sold nearly all the Nez Percés's country. My father was not there. He said to me: "When you go into council with the white man, always remember your country. Do not give it away. The white man will cheat you out of your home. I have taken no pay from the United States. I have never sold our land." In this treaty Lawyer acted without authority from our band. He had no right to sell the Wallowa [*winding water*] country. That had always belonged to my father's own people, and the other bands had never disputed our right to it. No other Indians ever claimed Wallowa.

In order to have all people understand how much land we owned, my father planted poles around it and said: "Inside is the home of my people—the white man may take the land outside. Inside this boundary all our people were born. It circles around the graves of our fathers, and we will never give up these graves to any man."

The United States claimed they had bought all the Nez Percés country outside of Lapwai Reservation, from Lawyer and other chiefs, but we continued to live in this land in peace until eight years ago, when white men began to come inside the bounds my father had set. We warned them against this great wrong, but they would not leave our land, and some bad blood was raised. The white men represented that we were going upon the warpath. They reported many things that were false.

The United States Government again asked for a treaty council. My father had become blind and feeble. He could no longer speak for his people. It was then that I took my father's place as chief.

In this council I made my first speech to white men. I said to the agent who held the council: "I did not want to come to this council, but I came hoping that we could save blood. The white man has no right to come here and take our country. We have never accepted any presents from the Government. Neither Lawyer nor any other chief had authority to sell this land. It has always belonged to my people. It came unclouded to them from our fathers, and we will defend this land as long as a drop of Indian blood warms the hearts of our men."

The agent said he had orders, from the Great White Chief at Washington, for us to go upon the Lapwai Reservation, and that if we obeyed he would help us in many ways. "You *must* move to the agency," he said. I answered him: "I will not. I do not need your help; we have plenty and we are contented and happy if the white man will let us alone. The reservation is too small for so many people with all their stock. You can keep your presents; we can go to your towns and pay for all we need; we have plenty of horses and cattle to sell, and we won't have any help from you; we are free now; we can go where we please. Our fathers were born here. Here they lived, here they died, here are their graves. We will never leave them." The agent went away, and we had peace for a little while.

Soon after this my father sent for me. I saw he was dying. I took his hand in mine. He said: "My son, my body is returning to my mother earth, and my spirit is going very soon to see the

Great Spirit Chief. When I am gone, think of your country. You are the chief of these people. They look to you to guide them. Always remember that your father never sold his country. You must stop your ears whenever you are asked to sign a treaty selling your home. A few years more, and white men will be all around you. They have their eyes on this land. My son, never forget my dying words. This country holds your father's body. Never sell the bones of your father and your mother." I pressed my father's hand and told him I would protect his grave with my life. My father smiled and passed away to the spirit-land.

I buried him in that beautiful valley of winding waters. I love that land more than all the rest of the world. A man who would not love his father's grave is worse than a wild animal.

For a short time we lived quietly. But this could not last. White men had found gold in the mountains around the land of winding water. They stole a great many horses from us, and we could not get them back because we were Indians. The white men told lies for each other. They drove off a great many of our cattle. Some white men branded our young cattle so they could claim them. We had no friend who would plead our cause before the law councils. It seemed to me that some of the white men in Wallowa were doing these things on purpose to get up a war. They knew that we were not strong enough to fight them. I labored hard to avoid trouble and bloodshed. We gave up some of our country to the white men, thinking that then we could have peace. We were mistaken. The white man would not let us alone. We could have avenged our wrongs many times, but we did not. Whenever the Government has asked us to help them against other Indians, we have never refused. When the white men were few and we were strong, we could have killed them all off, but the Nez Percés wished to live at peace.

If we have not done so, we have not been to blame. I believe that the old treaty has never been correctly reported. If we ever owned the land we own it still, for we never sold it. In the treaty councils the commissioners have claimed that our country had been sold to the Government. Suppose a white man should come to me and say, "Joseph, I like your horses, and I want to buy them." I say to him, "No, my horses suit me, I will not sell them." Then he goes to my neighbor, and says to him: "Joseph has some good horses. I want to buy them, but he refuses to sell." My neighbor answers, "Pay me the money, and I will sell you Joseph's horses." The white man returns to me, and says, "Joseph, I have bought your horses, and you must let me have them." If we sold our lands to the Government, this is the way they were bought.

CHIEF JOSEPH, *Nez Percé*

· 4 ·
We Are Not Children

Inviting Native American chiefs to journey to the national capital to meet the "Great White Father," as they termed the President, was a ritual as old as the Republic itself. Ever since George Washington asked the Iroquois leaders Cornplanter, Red Jacket, Farmer's Brother, and Captain Joseph Brant to visit Philadelphia in 1792, the excursion had appealed to the Indians' respect for pomp and protocol. The visits also gave the government a fine opportunity for impressing Indians with the power and might of white civilization before they sat down at the conference table.

In the fall of 1873, a delegation of Otoe chiefs from Nebraska

Medicine Horse.

held discussions with the Commissioner of Indian Affairs and their own agent in Washington, D.C. Foremost on the minds of the Otoes was permission for a final buffalo hunt and approval to relocate their tribe in Indian Territory in Oklahoma. Two of the chiefs, Medicine Horse and Stand By, had been in the city nineteen years earlier, when the Otoe signed the last six treaties they made with the government of the United States.

Just before this second trip, the superintendent of the Otoe reservation in Nebraska had written to his colleagues in Washington: "I cannot account for the ardent desire of all Indians with whom I have had business relations to visit the City of Washington. It appears to be the Mecca of their hopes. The Otoes have been particularly anxious to go there."

As the following condensation of a handwritten transcript of the conversations dramatizes, Washington was no Mecca this time around. The Otoe chiefs came away from the talks fully aware of the helpless status earlier treaties had placed them in. The Commissioner, Edward P. Smith, shocks them with his reading of a paragraph in the treaty reserving to the President the right to decide how the Otoes are to use the money owed them for the land they had agreed to sell. The frustrating exchange also communicates the flavor of official attitudes toward Native Americans at this time.

A year after these conversations Medicine Horse attempted to lead fifty families on a flight to freedom from their Nebraska reservation into Kansas Territory, but he was shortly captured and imprisoned.

October 31, 1873,
First Day

COMMISSIONER: I am glad to see you, my friends, as representatives of your tribe in Nebraska and hear what you have to say and render of your desires. Your tribe is an important one. You are elderly men, and probably have children, and what you say today will not only be for today, but will live after you.

MEDICINE HORSE: Grandfather, I have wanted to see you. We did not come for nothing, but we are tired. We just came. We want to ask one thing, whether you have done it or not. Before I left my tribe wanted to go on a buffalo hunt, and waited for permission from their Grandfather. We want to know if it has been sent.

COMMISSIONER: Your Agent asked a short time ago for permission for you to go on a hunt, and he stated that it was necessary, for you to get something to eat. We thought a long time before we decided what to do, as it is bad for Indians to go on a hunt. This strikes you as very strange. It is because we must do one thing or the other. Either let you continue wild as you now are, or make you like white men; and nothing keeps up this wild living like hunting. No white man could hunt as you do, and farm. No one can take care of himself and do it. Now because we are not ready to help you and put you where you can help yourself, it is decided to let you go on the hunt. Now is there something else?

MEDICINE HORSE: Grandfather, I have to say the same I said before. Grandfather should listen to what we said before. He has been living here all the time. We just came. Give us time.

COMMISSIONER: We will not talk anymore today then. You will think a long time and then you will talk well.

November 1, 1873,
Second Day

COMMISSIONER: Yesterday when we met you were tired and could not talk. I hope you have had a good sleep and can talk well now.

MEDICINE HORSE: My tribe has sent me down here to do the talking for them. I spoke to our Agent about it and I suppose you have heard about it, that we would sell our land. All our white brothers have big pieces of land, and get along much better than we do. We want the same. Some of the chiefs went with me to see another country. I like it and want to go there.

COMMISSIONER: There are two kinds of Indians there. Some

are good and work, and others are very wild and bad. I should be very sorry to have you go from Nebraska so as to be able to go wild again like some now in Indian Territory. What you ought to do is get ready as fast as you can to be like white people, and know as much as they do. There are white men who live by roaming about, but they do not amount to much.

STAND BY: I made a Treaty and sold our lands—a large piece of it. We did not sell it for paper money but for hard money.

COMMISSIONER: I will tell you now for what purpose this money was promised to you. The Treaty says that all this money [the Commissioner picks up a volume of treaties and reads] is to be "expended for your use and benefit under the direction of the President of the United States who may from time to time (that means from year to year) determine at his discretion what proportion of the annual payments shall be paid in money and what portion shall be spent in your education, for such beneficial objects as in his judgment shall advance them in civilization, for building, opening farms, fencing, breaking land, providing stock, agricultural implements, seed, clothing, etc." That is what the money is given for. The President decides whether to give the money or other things which he considers better for you. I will not take your money away but will spend it so as to do you good. Four hundred dollars will feed your tribe a month. It will fence a farm that will feed you and your children a hundred years. Is it not better for us to send money to your Agent to fence your farms than to send it to you to pass over to traders for trinkets?

STAND BY: We always raised something from the ground to support our families before we ever saw white men. But sometimes we get a good many furs and they bring us more money than we can get from what we raise. My Father told me if I wanted anything I should come here and get it. I know what kind of a treaty we made. I have it in my head.

COMMISSIONER: Things last longer on paper than they do in

your head. Your grandchildren will be able to take from this paper what was agreed to be done with the money. When they couldn't tell at all from your head better than you can now.

STAND BY: How would these white men feel to have their property used in this way?

COMMISSIONER: If the white men are children and you are their guardian, you can do what you please with their money—provided you do what is good for them.

MEDICINE HORSE: We are not children. We are men. I never thought I would be treated so when I made the Treaty.

COMMISSIONER: I have no way of knowing what was said at the time of the making of the Treaty, but to read what is written on the paper on which you have put your mark. If this course I propose was injuring you I should not propose it. But it is for your own good.

MEDICINE HORSE: Father, look at me and not at the table.

COMMISSIONER: I am busy writing.

MEDICINE HORSE: Those black curly-haired people I have always heard were made free. I thought I was always a free man. I am free yet. It hurts me badly what you read in the book. I did not know it was there.

COMMISSIONER: Did the Great Father promise always to do all you wanted him to do?

MEDICINE HORSE: We will not talk anymore now. We will think about it.

November 4, 1873, Third Day

COMMISSIONER: You have had a good long time to think about what we are to talk of today.

MEDICINE HORSE: Father, what you said to us the other day

hurt our feelings very much and we could not sleep since. When we made a trade, they did not tell us we must use our money, as you told us the other day. Our Great Father owes us a great deal of money. I always thought I should draw my money. Your talk the other day takes our rights away. I will be ashamed to take home this news.

STAND BY: I can not say anything different from what this fellow has been saying. I have been living a long time up there on the reservation, but we have got dissatisfied. Before we started, we had a council between ourselves. Our plan suited us. Your plan does not suit us at all.

COMMISSIONER: Our Great Father likes his children and does what is best for them when sometimes his children do not like it. You have received these annuities for nearly twenty years. You have had the best land in Nebraska. Just such land as your white brothers have made such good homes out of. Now why is it you have no houses, oxen, cows, horses, and homes like the white man? You have not been brought up that way. But there is a change coming over your life and it is hard for an old man to change his ways, but unless you change sometime, and it is hard for some old ones, it will be hard for the children to change.

STAND BY: We don't want to settle this business now. We want to go home and study about it. When white men want to make a plan, they get together and study about it two or three days. You want to put it all through at once, like drowning me in the river. We are not the only chiefs. There are some more at home. We will take the news home, and if it suits all, we will have to do so.

COMMISSIONER: There is no use to talk about half the land for that is settled. Congress passed a law and you all agreed to it, and men have been sent out to appraise the land, and if there is anyone to buy it, the land will be sold.

STAND BY: If you have a piece of land and I sell it, you would not like it.

COMMISSIONER: If you are my Agent and sell it, it is all right. You must remember there is a difference. You are the child of Government, and it must take care of you.

STAND BY: If you have children and they want money, they have it. They do as they want to.

COMMISSIONER: No, they do not. My child does as I want to have her. If any child wants anything and I want her to have it she gets it. But if I don't want her to have it she don't get it and she does not turn around and ask me how I would like it if she had my money and would not let me have it.

BIG BEAR: We work all the time. We like to work. You want to bind us right down, and we don't like it. I have raised wheat, corn, potatoes, and pumpkins. We all work. But you cannot make white men of us. That is one thing you can't do.

MEDICINE HORSE: I don't want to sell part of the reservation.

COMMISSIONER: Half of your reservation will be sold and tell your people so when you go home or you will tell them a falsehood. Now we have talked enough today.

STAND BY: You must not get tired of us. We have much to say.

COMMISSIONER: You are rightly named Stand By.

STAND BY: The Railroad gave us money for the right of way through our Territory and it is here, and we would like it.

AGENT: They sold the right of way through the Reservation for nineteen hundred dollars and the Agent before me arranged for one thousand dollars to be spent for provisions which he turned over to me, and I expended that amount last summer. And there must be some one thousand dollars still on hand.

MEDICINE HORSE: We did not order you to buy any cattle or horses for us.

COMMISSIONER: You did not need to. You are my children,

and I had a right to buy what I wanted to for you. It takes you a long time to find out that I am going to do what I think best for you.

MEDICINE HORSE: There is such a thing as children being whipped too often.

COMMISSIONER: There is a little over nine hundred dollars left you on the account of the railroad lands.

INTERPRETER: They want to keep that for provisions this winter. They are afraid they will not have a good hunt.

COMMISSIONER: I will send it to the Agent to spend for you in pork and flour.

MEDICINE HORSE: When I came here to visit the Great Father, he always gave us money to buy presents for our children.

COMMISSIONER: The Great Father never did that. The first time he ever did was to those Crows, and he is not going to do so anymore. But I will give you some presents to give the chiefs who did not come. I want you to go and see the President tomorrow at his house and in the afternoon go to the Navy yard and see the guns and shops and ships if you would like to.

MEDICINE HORSE, ET AL., *Otoe*

· 5 ·

Plenty Coups
Travels to Washington

To Indians from the Far West much of the adventure of an official visit to Washington lay in the long journey. The first Crow Indian delegation to visit the city left central Montana in 1872, rode on horseback to Salt Lake City, then embarked

on the train. In 1880 a second group went East to discuss
a railroad that was to cut across Crow lands. Among the chiefs
was a rising young leader named Plenty Coups, who later de-
scribed it.

They said they were going to take me to Washington. I thought
it over for a while. I thought it was a wise thing. I told them
I would go. This was my first trip east. I also told them that I
wanted some other chiefs to go with me. I asked Two-Belly. At
first he didn't want to go, but finally he said he would. The
others were Old Crow, Pretty Eagle, Long Elk, and Medicine
Crow. Three white men also accompanied us: A. M. Quivey,
Tom Stewart, and J. R. Keller.

It was during the spring. There was no railroad yet in our
country, and we had to travel by stagecoach which carried a
light at night. We traveled in two coaches. Snow was still lying
on the ground. We set out from the old agency, near Flesh
Scraper Mountain. The horses were relayed, but we had no
rest during these changes of horses. We traveled toward Butte
[Montana], which took us four nights and five days. The
further we came into the mountains, the deeper lay the snow.
At Butte we rested for the first time. We slept a whole day
and night. And I combed my hair for the first time since leaving
our camp.

Early the next morning we were told to dress quickly and eat.
The teams were ready and we traveled down the mountain, following Flathead River. Again we were relayed. We continued
until we came close to another mountain, and we saw an Indian
driving some horses. We called him to us. He was a Bannock.
We asked him where the Bannocks were. He told us that they
were on the other side of the mountain, in the valley. He also

told us that their chief, Comes Out of the Grease, had gone to Washington. . . .

Early the next morning we took a sweatbath with the Bannocks. They told us that the road from their camp to the next station was hard and rough, and that it was better to travel by daytime. At that station, however, we should see the Fast Wagon [train]. They described it as a big black horse with his belly nearly touching the ground. This horse had a big bell on his back. He ran so fast that everytime he stopped, he puffed.

We left about noon and came to a big barn after dark where we slept. Early the next morning we started again and found the snow deep. Soon it started to rain which made the roads even worse. It was again after dark before we stopped at a dugout town, where they were building the railroad. Here we had supper. A white man with us pointed to a clock and told us that when the hands should be in a certain position we should start again. We did not know what he meant. Next morning we were awakened, took our bundles, and were taken to the train. We walked into the cars and sat down. We placed our bundles on shelves and looked out of the window. The train followed the river. Through the windows we could see many horses, game, and mountains. Stewart, who was traveling with us, acted as interpreter. We arrived at the Bannock Agency, and many Indians were there. As soon as the train stopped, we wanted to get off, but we were told to stay. That black horse was panting so hard that the bell on his neck was ringing.

We thought the train journey was grand. I realized, however, that it was not a horse that pulled it, and I wondered what made it go so fast. Birds would fly along outside our windows. They were swift, but before long we outdistanced them.

We had often been told that the Sioux were a numerous tribe. But it seemed to me that the Bannock was even larger. We halted at a junction, and another train passed going in a

The 1880 Crow delegation to Washington. Plenty Coups is seated in the front row (second from the right).

different direction. I saw a lake with a mountain rising from its center. We saw many white man's places, and passed many freshly-skinned elk and buffalo carcasses. . . .

We came to a big forest and passed it and finally we arrived at the Missouri. Here we met a white man called Wood Frost who had been our agent. He invited us to dinner and gave us some red paint and shells. We had not even finished our meal when we had to leave for the train. We crossed the Missouri and were told that we were going to Chicago.

It was the first time that I had seen so many white people together. It was strange to see so many tall black houses. Here we left the train. There was a big lake and we spent much time there watching the ice bump against the shore and break into pieces. It was the biggest ice breakup I had ever seen, and the waves were very high.

There was more travel by train and finally we arrived in Washington. Here wagons were ready waiting for us. They took us to our lodging, and we were told to sleep until the next morning when we should be taken to President Hayes. The next day we were escorted to the President, who shook hands with us and told us that he was glad to see us. The President said that he had sent for us to talk concerning the future of our people. He said that he wanted us to send our children to school and that they would build a house and barn for each of us. He wanted us to learn how to farm. He said they were going to build a railroad through the Yellowstone Valley, but that they wanted us to make peace with the other tribes in our part of the country.

My companions told me to make some reply so I said that we were also glad to see him and that we wished to speak with him too. I said that he had asked us to do many things, but that before we could give him our answer, we would like time to talk it over among ourselves. The President gave us two days to consider his requests. Two days later we returned and again met with him. I said that we agreed to send our children to school and to let the Government build houses for us. I said that as far as stopping the fighting with other tribes, we wanted to fight them for about two more years and then we would reconsider this question. I added that we did not want a railroad built through our country because it was our hunting ground.

When we said this, the President kept us in Washington for over a month. We had several conferences with him in which he tried to overrule our objections, but he failed. The President suggested giving us another hunting ground, in North Dakota, but I refused because we did not wish to leave our country. When the President asked my reasons I said that in North Dakota the mountains are low and that I wanted to live where the mountains are high and where they are many springs of fresh water.

Then the President asked how we had treated the soldiers, and I said that we had been friendly to them. When their horses feet were sore, so were ours. When they had to drink alkali, we shared their misfortune. When they suffered, we suffered, and I said we would continue to have friendly relations. Then the President said that he would grant our request to remain in the country where we lived, but that in return he expected us to let them build a railroad through the valley of the Yellowstone.

I said that when I returned to my people I would talk with them and hear their objections. I said then he could send us one of his servants and we would hold a council with him and he would tell the President of the results.

We were in Washington a long time. I became anxious to return home and see my people again. The President told us that we could return home in two Sundays. Although we dreaded the long journey, we were glad. When the day arrived, we again walked into the cars and traveled for a long time. It was late summer when we finally reached home, but the trees were still in full leaf.

Soon after we returned, we had a conference with the railroad and government officials. We finally agreed to let them build the railroad through our country, and they agreed to give us free transportation. This was done at first, but soon this agreement was not lived up to and since then we have had to pay for our own transportation. A few years later the Government began to build homes for the Crows on the Big Horn River. I then went to Pryor [the westernmost town on the Crow Indian reservation]. I donated the use of four head of horses and had a log house built on the land where I live today.

PLENTY COUPS, Crow

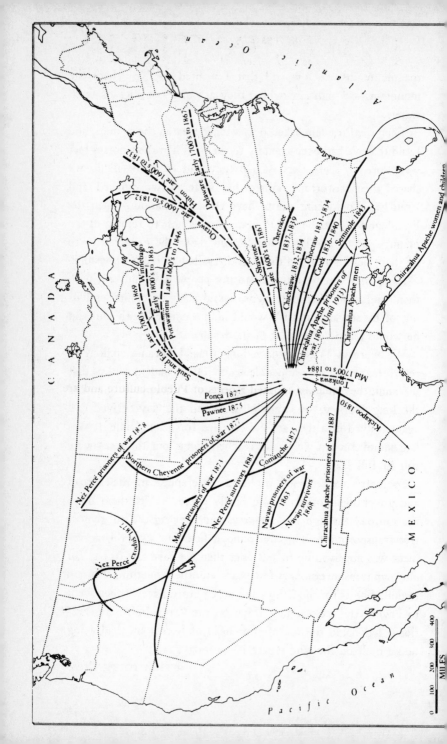

EXILES IN THEIR OWN LAND

Long before they were driven from their homes by an expanding white society, many Native American peoples could have told of tribal resettlements. In the fourteenth century some Siouan-speaking groups are believed to have undertaken an incredible journey from what we know today as the Carolinas to Minnesota, where they established themselves as the eastern Sioux. Sometime in the fifteenth century bands of Athapascan-speaking people from the north entered present-day New Mexico; they quickly adopted aspects of Pueblo culture and are known today as the nation's largest tribe, the Navajo. In the late seventeenth century a clan of Missouri River Hidatsa broke away and traveled westward to become the Montana Crow. Not many decades later the Kiowa began an odyssey that took them from the northern to the southern Great Plains where they adopted new cultural patterns. These and other large migrations generally occurred over a sufficient period of time so that the emigrants could gradually adapt to their new surroundings and new neighbors.

But the relentless spread of white culture throughout America

Native American peoples were displaced from their ancestral homelands through wars, treaties, and takeovers of their lands by white settlers. The map shows the approximate routes and dates of some of these removals; the broken lines indicate the more gradual displacements that took place over a period of time. Indian Territory, which consisted of most of the present-day state of Oklahoma, became a melting pot for peoples from every part of the United States. (BERNHARD H. WAGNER) allowed no such periods of grace. The series of convulsive tribal displacements that began soon after Native American contact with whites seriously disrupted Indian life everywhere. Generation after generation of Native American families came to know only the sorrows and terrors of exile. All their worldly goods on their backs, the Indian refugees suffered harassment from unfriendly whites along the way. Starvation and disease were their constant companions as they walked along unfamiliar roads to country they had never seen. Sometimes friendly Indians gave them shelter; sometimes enemy tribes took the opportunity to attack them.

Although these tribal uprootings reached their peak in the 1830's, they had acquired a customary pattern long before, and they continued until the end of the nineteenth century. "I think you had better put the Indians on wheels," a Sioux named Red Dog bitterly complained to treaty commissioners in 1876. "Then you can run them about whenever you wish."

The story of this erratic shifting of Native American populations begins in the mid-seventeenth century, when the Iroquois, making the most of their strategic balance-of-power position between England and France, routed the Hurons westward. They then forced the Sauk and Fox, Osage, and Potawatomi into the uninhabited, northern Mississippi Valley. In the Southeast, white settlement compelled tribes to abandon their riverbank camps and seek refuge in the deep woods. In 1704 the English rampage against the Indians in Florida contributed to the formation of a new Native American tribe: the fleeing Creek regrouped as the Seminole Indians of the Everglades—the name Seminole means "runaway."

Between 1750 and 1850 the Osage averaged a hundred miles of westward movement every ten years. And in 1886 the Delaware chief Journeycake mournfully recollected his people's reluctant

transformation into nomads: "We have been broken up and removed six times. We have been despoiled of our property. We
thought when we moved across the Missouri River and paid for
our homes in Kansas we were safe, but in a few years the white
man wanted our country." Eventually nearly every Indian nation
would be reduced to frontier flotsam by this push-and-shove
movement toward the setting sun.

In the latter part of the eighteenth century, once the victorious
American colonists no longer felt obliged to woo Indian allies in
their struggle against England, they began eying Indian lands,
particularly in the Southeast where settlers were shortly crowd-
ing as "thick as grass"—as the Indians phrased it. After 1790
the United States government faced four options in shaping its
overall policy toward Indians: (1) exterminate them; (2) protect
them in zoolike enclaves while towns rise around them; (3)
assimilate Indians by encouraging them to become crop-raising,
church-going, school-attending model citizens; (4) transplant
them to that inhospitable, unwanted wilderness west of the
Mississippi, known as Indian Territory.

President Thomas Jefferson had argued that assimilation was
the only moral course. But in 1803, the year the United States
acquired the Louisiana Purchase from France, thus gaining that
vast expanse of land stretching from the Mississippi River to the
Rocky Mountains, even Jefferson suggested that perhaps the
Indians might be "safer" if relocated in this new territory.

Over the next forty years, largely due to clamor from the
citizens of Georgia, and of the newly created states of Tennessee,
Alabama, and Mississippi, this policy of removal would reign.
Of all the treaties signed with the Indians, none had such
anguishing consequences as the seventy-six prescribing wholesale emigration as the final solution to the Indian problem. During
the period of intensive removals—from 1816 to 1850—over a

hundred thousand Native Americans from twenty-eight tribes would be deported west of "the Great Waters" (the Mississippi). As the waves of these and later groups came westward, the newcomers sometimes met with resentment from the culturally different Indian peoples in their way. Warfare between them and the western Indians over shrinking food supplies broke out as early as 1816.

The southeastern removals began about 1811 when a trickle of Cherokee from Tennessee were persuaded to resettle. But that exodus did not satisfy the Southern States, especially Georgia where gold had been discovered. White cotton growers were also impatient to cultivate the fertile Indiana fields. Homesteaders in Arkansas and Missouri began haranguing the federal authorities to quit stalling and clear all Indians from the area. Abruptly the Southern States outlawed the new tribal governments. This was painfully ironic since at least four of the South's so-called Five Civilized Tribes—Cherokee, Choctaw, Chickasaw, and Creek— had responded to President Jefferson's earlier advice to assimilate. Proud of their recently drafted laws and constitutions, their trimly tilled fields, and well-bred herds, their slaves, grist mills, and missionary schools, they were successfully emulating white culture while giving it an unmistakably Indian cast. Yet no matter how well the Civilized Tribes blended white and Indian worlds, the federal government began caving in to state pressure to remove them all. Before long the once vast "Indian Territory" would be reduced to the confines of the present-day state of Oklahoma.

Shortly after his inauguration in 1829, President Andrew Jackson, who had never hidden his scorn for Native American rights, publicly refused to honor federal treaty obligations to protect the southern tribes from harassment by vigilantes or from trespass by squatters on their ancestral lands. In the spring of 1830, Jackson's Indian Removal Act was finally passed by Congress. Now, the President (whom the Indians had named "Sharp Knife") had both the power to select the tribes that were to be removed and the money—half a million dollars—to finance the giant exodus. To present an illusion of tribal consent, Jackson's secret agents bribed, deceived, and intimidated individual Indians, falsified records, squelched open debate, and finally persuaded some tribesmen to sign in favor of removal.

Digging in against removal, the Cherokee quarrel with the state of Georgia went all the way to the United States Supreme Court. In 1831 the tribe finally won an unequivocal acknowledgement of their status as an independent sovereign nation. In the historic opinion of Chief Justice John Marshall, the "acts of Georgia are repugnant to the Constitution. . . . They are in direct hostility with treaties [which] . . . solemnly pledge the faith of the United States to restrain their citizens from trespassing on it [Cherokee territory]. . . ." But Chief Justice Marshall's significant decision notwithstanding, President Jackson and Georgia officials were determined to oust the tribe.

The Cherokee resistance to removal was tirelessly led by a part-Cherokee named John Ross. Ross and his followers refused in 1835 to sign the illegal Treaty of New Echota, in which a fraction of the tribe agreed to go west. The debate over removal caused bloody disputes within the Cherokee community. Opponents of Ross said his stand was unrealistic, and later charged that the position he had taken caused greater hardship for the Cherokee when removal ultimately came. A leading advocate of Cherokee rights for more than forty years, Ross continued to defend his people when they resettled in Indian Territory and successfully rebuilt their dislocated lives and institutions.

The Choctaw were the first to make the hard journey. Leaving their Mississippi farms in the winter of 1831, several groups

John Ross in a photograph taken in 1862, four years before his death.
(NEBRASKA STATE HISTORICAL SOCIETY, LINCOLN)

began the long trek westward under guard only to meet a blizzard of snow and below-zero weather; many of the Choctaw were barefoot and starving, one blanket being allotted to each family. The Creek began leaving Alabama in 1836—"drove off like wolves," as they described it—many of them in chains. A rotting, overloaded steamboat bearing one group sank, drowning 311 men, women, and children. Nearly half the Creek nation died either en route or during their first years in the harsh, unfamiliar climate of Oklahoma. In 1837, the first of the Cherokee began their nation's two-year-long removal, a time the Cherokee still refer to as "the drive-away."

Rebecca Nuegin was a three-year-old Cherokee child when her family's ordeal began. "When the soldiers came to our house," she recalled as an old woman, "my father wanted to fight, but my mother told him that the soldiers would kill him if he did, and we surrendered without a fight. They drove us out of the house to join other prisoners in a stockade."

Traveling west in three separate parties, the Cherokee lost a quarter of their tribe to sickness and exposure. An estimated thirty thousand Native Americans perished either on these tragic journeys or shortly thereafter during the lawless period of readjustment in Indian Territory where the surviving members of over sixty dislocated tribes eventually came to live.

Still another series of removals occurred in the Ohio Valley, where tribes who had already undergone at least one uprooting were pressured to sign new agreements to travel yet again to alien soil. In the 1850's and 60's, the removal idea lay behind the displacement of tribes in the Far West as well. Indeed the sufferings of exile were experienced by Native Americans as far apart as California, the Great Lakes, and the Southwest.

The Choctaw still tell a story that poignantly sums up the profound sense of loss felt by the many Native Americans who were forced to leave their homelands. As one Choctaw community was about to move from its ancestral Mississippi forest and start the westward trek to Indian Territory, the women made a formal procession through the trees surrounding their abandoned cabins, stroking the leaves of the oak and elm trees in silent farewell. In each of the episodes that follow, we see tribal worlds threatened with the next worst calamity to extermination.

· 1 ·
Plea from the Chickasaw

When United States government officials suggested in 1826 that the Chickasaw swap their Tennessee Valley hamlets for unseen territory west of the Mississippi River, the Chickasaw leaders responded as follows.

Actually the Chickasaw had quietly begun moving west as early as 1822. After the removal treaties of 1832 and 1834 were signed, the remainder of the tribe followed, taking along five thousand of their highly prized horses. Although they had to slog their way through swamps and continually fight off horse thieves, their journey was better planned and financed than the other Southeast removals. The Chickasaw arrived in Indian Territory considerably less damaged in body and spirit than the Creek, Cherokee, and Choctaw.

We never had a thought of exchanging our land for any other, as we think that we would not find a country that would suit us as well as this we now occupy, it being the land of our fore-fathers, if we should exchange our lands for any other, fearing the consequences may be similar to transplanting an old tree, which would wither and die away, and we are fearful we would come to the same. . . .

We have no lands to exchange for any other. We wish our father [the President] to extend his protection to us here, as he proposes to do on the west of the Mississippi, as we apprehend we would, in a few years, experience the same difficulties in any other section of the country that might be suitable to us west of the Mississippi. . . .

Our father the President wishes that we should come under

the laws of the United States; we are a people that are not enlightened, and we cannot consent to be under your Government. If we should consent, we should be likened unto young corn growing and met with a drought that would kill it.

LEVI COLBERT, ET AL., *Chickasaw*

· 2 ·

Tushpa Crosses the Mississippi

Between 1800 and 1830, white men tried on more than forty occasions to force the Choctaw to sell their Mississippi homeland. By 1830 the tribe had given up more than thirteen million acres. Nonetheless, pressure to yield the remaining ten million acres continued. Finally, when the Treaty of Dancing Rabbit Creek was signed in September 1830, most of the Choctaw agreed to move west.

Tushpa, who was later to provide his son, James Culberson, with the following account of the band's ordeal, was then about twelve years old. Carrying their worldly goods on their backs, this clan was among the very last to leave. Their journey began in early spring 1834, and took them to Skullyville Agency, established the year before, in eastern Oklahoma. During the entire Choctaw removal, two thousand out of the twenty thousand who left their homes in Mississippi died. Intimate reminiscences of the removal period, such as Tushpa's story, are extremely rare, as if even the memories were too painful to recall.

This particular band consisted of about one hundred persons, men, women, and children, and were all full-blood Choctaw Indians of very small means, and in fact had nothing of value to help them make this trip. The captain or headman of this band arranged the order of travel. One man was selected to carry choice seed corn for the planting of new fields; another to choose and select seeds from choice peach and apple trees so that new orchards might be planted; another to choose and select choice beans and melon seeds for the new gardens. . . .

Only a partial list of those who went in this band is necessary for us to know: Tushpa, the bare-footed lad; Ishtona, the deliverer, the mother of Tushpa; Kanchi, the seller, the father of Tushpa; Ishtaya, the fire bearer; Halbi, the kicker, second chief; and Chilita, the wise daughter of Halbi. . . .

Kanchi, who had heard a missionary preach from what he told the Indians through interpretation was a book from God, called his brethren together in the camp, and while the news of the disaster of the burning of their homes was fresh on their minds, and some swearing vengeance and others for giving up all and resigning to fate, bade them listen to him.

He said: "My own kin and blood brothers, I know how you feel about what has happened to you; I too have felt the same and looked about for comfort from this wretchedness into which we have been brought. . . . Why are we surrounded by foes and cast out of our homes. . . ? Some time back beyond our old homes I heard a man preach from a book that he called a Bible [*Holisso Holitopa*], and although that book was read by a white man, I believe there is something better in it than the way the white man acts. . . . We are in much trouble now, but don't want to kill or destroy, so give us hearts that we hear about in this book and let us be good, and if we live to see this new country to which we travel, help some of us to do good to those we meet. Perhaps we will not bring shame upon the land."

It was now early spring of 1834, and the Mississippi River was carrying a larger amount of headwater this spring than usual so it was necessary to wait until the river had fallen in its flow so that it could be crossed.

The party put up some shelter and arranged temporary camps and prepared to stay on the banks of the river until they might cross it. On the second night of their stay a runner had announced that a fire had destroyed their former homes and everything that had been left in them, so that the last hope of remaining in this homeland was rudely snatched away. . . .

Chief Baha ordered that arrangements be made for the crossing; so a plan to use a raft made of logs to carry over a part of the baggage and make a quicker crossing was agreed upon. . . . The point at which the party crossed is in the southeastern part of Arkansas in Desha County at the mouth of Cypress Creek south of Friars Point. The river here is about one mile wide and has a pretty stiff current at low tide. . . . An island known as Bihi or Mulberry Island was near the middle of the stream and broke the swift current of the main river and was used as a place to rest and straighten the cargo. . . .

Baha, the chief headman, had often made this crossing to visit some Indians who lived over the river near the Big Mound, and told his people they could make an easy crossing as he knew all the currents and landing places. During the two weeks' delay a number of small canoes and one large raft of logs were made by the men. . . .

Four canoes with four men in each were used to pull the raft loaded with household goods, clothing, and other things to be carried or used in the journey, and also some persons, men, women and children, were shipped over as each raftload made the crossing. . . . an accident happened when it appeared that the success in crossing would be complete. The raft was being towed across on its fifth trip laden with people and goods, when it was struck by a swiftly moving submerged tree. . . .

In the excitement, Kanchi, who was on duty as a guard, after rescuing two children and balancing the raft, in some manner became entangled in the swirling, twisting mass of brush, trees, and refuse, and caught in the undertow, never came to the surface again. . . . Some thought of going no farther on the journey but realized it was impractical now as half of the party had already crossed over the river. Others recalled the prayer that Kanchi had made for them. . . .

The final crossing was made after a week of hard work, and the party decided to rest for a few days before attempting the westward journey and accordingly made a temporary camp upon the high ground away from the river bank. It had been six weeks since leaving their homes, and a greater part of the time there had been occasional rains, and not having had proper shelter, the aged people and young children had begun to show signs of the exposure which they had encountered. As a result of the weather an old lady and three small children died. . . .

A few days after these funeral rites were performed the headman, Baha, issued orders. . . . The march was resumed and much hard work was done to overcome the difficulties they now encountered. The trail now led through a dense forest. . . . Something had to be done about it, so Baha called the headmen in a council, and it was finally decided to have a gang of men under a subchief go ahead and clear the trail about one day in advance of the marching clan.

This proved a wise plan as this gang also prepared rafts on the bayous and rivers, and no time was lost when the clan reached these streams . . . the march was continued and persisted in once they had left the high grounds near the Mississippi River, as the headmen had been informed that dry grounds and an open country was theirs to enjoy if once they could get through these swamps. Ten miles was ordered for a day's journey, and all, young and old alike, set their program to make the ten miles at any cost.

The first three days were the most disagreeable they were to experience as it was nearly all swamps, sometimes knee-deep in muck, and added to that, camp had to be made in these swamps and on damp grounds, and they often had to sleep in wet clothes.

Brush was piled up and made a very comfortable place to sleep. If only a good fire had been built and a good meal cooked, their bodies would have been revived in condition to carry on. But the emergency was urgent, and no conveniences were to be had. . . .

Having crossed the most dense swamps, the marchers located on dry ground and prepared a camp, where they remained a few days looking after the sick. . . . By slow, painful marches they at last reached Little Rock, Arkansas, on the fifteenth of May, 1834, having been on the road two and a half months already and only about one-half of the journey complete. . . .

Many complaints of sickness were heard in the camp, and Baha thought it best to move camp as it might renew the spirit of the people. So after having been at the Post [Little Rock] one week, they began the march on the Post road towards their final destination, Fort Smith, Arkansas, and Skullyville, in Indian Territory, fifteen miles west of Fort Smith, Arkansas. . . . Three days out of Little Rock an Indian boy, named Shunka, died from a sort of dysentery and it quickly spread in camp among the weakened ones, and in the course of a week, before the disease could be checked, three others died. . . . They were laid away near one of the camps and the funeral rites performed over their lovely resting places. . . . [Then] good progress was made towards Dardenelle on the Arkansas River, which they reached on the 30th of May.

A ferry boat was used here in crossing the river by the post service, and after some parleying, the owners of the ferry consented to take all the company free of charge and ask the United States government to pay the bill at some future time. . . .

Having crossed the Arkansas River on the 31st day of May, the route of the company was over a somewhat traveled road, but there were many hills to climb and the road was so hard and dry that many suffered. . . . The number of sick increased and a forced camp was made in the hills ten miles out from Dardenelle, Arkansas. . . . The medicine men waited upon them as best they could, but two more died at this camp. . . .

If they could reach Fort Smith, Arkansas, or Skullyville, all their wants would be supplied by the United States agent, but they were fifty miles away now. A council of the headmen was called and a plan was agreed to make a camp for the sick and have members to remain and nurse them and the able-bodied ones to go on to their destination . . . [Baha] called off the names of twenty-five additional ones [people to join the twenty-five who already agreed to go on ahead] and insisted that they go. . . . Some of those who went at this time met friends of former days and settled in the various parts of the Indian Territory. . . .

Baha having conducted them safely into Indian Territory, returned at once with provisions to the sick camp. Conditions had become worse and some had died during his absence and so many were sick that a near panic had taken place. . . . In this extremity the deaths reached a total of eight, a staggering toll for such a small group of people. Ishtona died during a storm in the night with Tushpa, Chilita, and other friends by her couch. . . . On the last night of their stay at this camp, Tushpa, Chilita, and Ishtaya visited the grave of Ishtona for a last *ai-aksho* [cry of mourning]. . . .

The remnant of this devoted company, weary, emaciated, and

penniless, reached the promised land, Indian Territory, on July 1st. At Skullyville they met real friends who took care of them and provided them with the necessary comforts for their immediate relief. Great rejoicing was experienced by them.

So ended a four-hundred-miles walk, one of the memorable migrations in the history of the native tribes in the United States. . . . After a few days' rest, the party so long together, separated to locate homes for themselves. Chilita remained near Skullyville with relatives. Ishtaya located a little further east of Skullyville near the Poteau River. He became a preacher. Later he and Chilita were married and moved across on the east side of the river, making a home at Pecola, where he was known as the famous preacher and evangelist—Willis Folsom. Their descendants occupy many places of trust in the state today. . . .

This, my fellow reader, is a true story of the life of John Culberson, or Tushpa, my father, a full-blood Choctaw Indian. . . . And who, on his death bed enjoined me to keep the family together and give them some chance for an education; to be a good citizen, and write the history of the journey if I thought it of benefit to mankind.

JAMES CULBERSON, *Choctaw*

· 3 ·

Corralling the Navajo

In the early years the Navajo of the Southwest were notorious marauders against the Spanish, Mexicans, and Pueblo Indians. Their first "peace and friendship" treaty with the government of the United States, signed in 1846, was supposed to quell any harassment of American settlers. But the Navajo were a widely spread people; there was no central authority over their wandering bands. Fifteen years, three unsuccessful military campaigns, and six treaties later, the word went out from Washington to round them all up.

Christopher "Kit" Carson headed the ruthless hunt in 1863–64, with ready help from the Ute and other Navajo enemies. His troops slaughtered Navajo sheep and cut down every Navajo cornstalk and fruit tree they came across. At last eighty-five-hundred starving men, women, and children were collected for the infamous "Long Walk," a 250-mile march to Bosque Redondo, near Fort Sumner, in eastern New Mexico. Here the Navajo were held in semiconfinement for four long years. Following their 1868 treaty with the United States they were, however, told they could return to their homeland near Fort Defiance, in Arizona; there they recuperated faster than most uprooted Indian tribes.

The events leading up to the Navajo removal are recollected here by Chester Arthur, clan relative of the most famous Navajo statesman of this century—Henry Chee Dodge.

About 1863, a Captain in the United States Army, called Red Shirt by the Indians, came to Red Lake, fifteen miles north of Fort Defiance, to make a treaty with the Navajos. He brought forty fat wethers for the feast and four big wagons loaded with calico, men's shirts and brass wire, to give away when the treaty was signed.

Red Shirt made a talk through his interpreter. He told the Indians they would have to stop stealing from the Mexicans, and from the neighboring tribes and each other. He told them they had made other treaties and broken them, but if they broke this

"Long Walk" of the Navajo, as drawn by the contemporary Navajo artist, Raymond Johnson. (NAVAJO COMMUNITY COLLEGE PRESS)

one, it would be the last. He and the head chiefs sat down together on a blanket and they said they would sign the treaty.

When they had all made their mark on the paper, he gave each of the ten chiefs a pair of pants, a big silver medallion of George Washington to be hung around their necks and a fine gold-headed cane. Then he told the rest of the Navajos to line up, and he would give them all presents from the wagons. They lined up, and he and his men began to issue the calico and wire and shirts, but when he looked behind him, he found the rest were stealing from the backs of the wagons.

The Indians grabbed the ends of bolts of calico and ran them out, cutting off long strips with their knives, and they took the brass wire and shirts until they stole all he had and were unharnessing the mules to steal them. These were all young men that the chiefs could not control and Red Shirt made another speech.

"I thank you, my friends," he said, "for accepting my gifts as a sign that you make this treaty. Now if you will leave me the empty wagons I will go back to Santa Fe and bring you four more loads of presents."

The Indians let him go with his mules, but after a while, Nahtahlith, the orator, got up and began a speech, in which he scolded them for their thievery. All the time they had been taking the calico and blankets he had covered his face for shame, and while he sat there he had a vision, for he was a prophet. He told the young men that when they died they would not go to join the spirits of their ancestors, those great warriors, but would become Indian devils and whirlwinds and blow about on earth. The white man would not come back with four wagons of presents to give them. He would reurn with many soldiers, and Mexicans and Zuñis and Utes and Moquis—all armed with guns to kill them.

The young Indians told him to shut up, they were tired of hearing him talk; but he told them he was making a prophecy. When they heard that, they kept still and he went on. For this stealing, he said, they would be punished by being driven out of the rich country where they were into the barren desert to the west, where there was no water and the land would not grow corn. They would run and hide, from place to place, and when they met some of their people they would say: "Where is my wife? Where is my father? Where are my children?"

But they would be hiding too, and the people would not

know. Many would starve, many more would be killed, and in all that rich valley by Red Lake there would not be a single Navajo—not even a moccasin track. Only the footprints of coyotes.

That frightened the young men and they fled, but the soldiers did not come back. At first the Navajos were afraid and watched the trails, but as summer came on with lots of rain they went back to their old homes and planted corn. Even around Fort Defiance, which the Indians had burned down, they planted more wheat than ever before. But just as it was ready to cut, Red Shirt and the soldiers came back.

All the Navajos ran away as the soldiers moved in and camped at the fort, for besides them there were many of their enemies, the Mexicans; and also many Utes and Zuñis, all with guns. But the ten chiefs who had signed the treaty stayed on the cliff above the fort, and one day they saw Red Shirt with his escort riding north on the old Indian trail. So they ran down quickly to where he would pass and laid their canes and pants and medallions in the road.

When Red Shirt came and saw the presents, he knew why the chiefs had left them and he hollered for them to come down. They were ashamed at first, but at last they came down and he asked them what these things meant.

"War," they said. "You have come back with your soldiers."

"Yes, my friends," he said, "it is war. But at the same time I want you to stay. Sit down and smoke tobacco with me today, and tomorrow we will fight. My Government has given orders to kill you all unless you come in and surrender. So come in to the fort today or else take your families and flee to the wildest mountains."

They smoked together, and he said: "I thank you, my friends, for trying to restrain your people from stealing. But there is only one way to do that now and tomorrow we begin to kill them."

He shook hands and the chiefs went away, and the next day the soldiers began. They rode out in small parties in every direction and killed all the Navajo sheep, goats, horses, and cows that they could find. They killed the herders with the sheep, little boys, and grown men, and chased them through the rocks. The soldiers took the wheat to feed their horses and mules and cut down all the corn. The Mexicans and Utes and Zuñis trailed the Navajos everywhere and robbed them and stole their women and children.

The Navajos went up into the Canyon de Chelly, but the Mexican soldiers followed them. They cut down their peach trees and corn and chased the Indians up over the rocks, so high that their bullets would not reach. Then they tried to starve them out. But the Navajos had taken many water bottles with them and had hidden lots of corn in the caves, and at night while the soldiers were asleep, they would slip down and bring back more water. It was very hot in the canyon, and the Captain of the soldiers died, so they took his body and went away.

Every day the Mexicans and Utes would ride out over the country, and whenever they found sheep or pony tracks, they would follow them and kill the herders. The rich Navajos who had many sheep and goats drove them west as far as Oraibi, where the Moqui [Hopi] villages are, and many went so far they took refuge in the bottom of the Grand Canyon. But now from every side other Indians came in to fight them. Even the Paiutes and the Apaches had been given guns to kill them and chased them clear into the wild mountains. All their crops were destroyed and when winter came the people began to starve.

But Nahtahlith, the prophet, did not wait to starve and die. When he left Fort Defiance he mounted his best horse and rode out to meet the Zuñis, who were marching up Wide Ruins Wash. They saw him coming and surrounded him. Then he rode down their line, shooting his arrows until he had killed four men. A Mexican hit him with a bullet, and as they ran in to finish him he said: "I thank you, my friends, for giving me a warrior's death."

"We thank you," they said, "for coming to be killed."

They filled him full of arrows and broke his arms and legs with rocks, taking the sinews out to make war medicine, for they had seen what a brave man he was.

The prophecy of Nahtahlith came true. Red Shirt was their good friend, but the young men would not listen to him. They were so bad that nothing could be done with them and so they were destroyed. Those who escaped were driven to the Grand Canyon and the Painted Desert, where they hid in the rocks like wild animals, but all except a few were rounded up and caught and taken away to Hwalte [Bosque Redondo].

CHESTER ARTHUR, *Navajo*

· 4 ·

The Uprooted Winnebago

Among the lesser-known stories of removal is that of the Wisconsin Winnebago. By 1865, when a chief named Little Hill told a Congressional investigating team about his people's most recent troubles, the Winnebago had been reluctant wanderers for some forty years. They had been pressured into signing seven land-turnover agreements and had changed location at least six times.

Evicted from their lead-rich lands along the Wisconsin River

in the 1820's, the Winnebago were jostled back and forth until
they finally agreed to settle in Minnesota. But, in the opinion
of their white neighbors, that land was far too good for them.
Under duress, they were sent to Crow Creek Reservation in
South Dakota, as Little Hill relates. But life there was so im-
poverished that most of the Winnebago either secretly returned
to Wisconsin or sought refuge with the Omaha in Nebraska,
where they were finally given the reservation that they occupy
to this day.

Formerly I did not live as I do now. We used to live in Minnesota. While we lived in Minnesota we used to live in good
houses, and always take our Great Father's advice and do whatever he told us to do. We used to farm and raise a crop of all we
wanted every year. While we lived there, we had teams of our
own. Each family had a span of horses or oxen to work, and had
plenty of ponies. Now, we have nothing. While we lived in
Minnesota another tribe of Indians committed depredations
against the whites [the 1862 Sioux uprising], and then we were
compelled to leave Minnesota. We did not think we would be
removed from Minnesota. Never expected to leave, and we were
compelled to leave so suddenly that we were not prepared,
not many could sell their ponies and things they had.

The superintendent of [our] farm was to take care of the
ponies we had left there and bring them on to us wherever we
went. But he brought to Crow Creek about fifty, and the rest
we do not know what became of them. Most all of us had put in
our crops that spring before we left, and we had to go and leave
everything but our clothes and household things. We had but
four days' notice. Some left their houses just as they were, with
their stoves and household things in them. They promised us

Two Cheyenne artists, Howling Wolf and Soaring Eagle, collaborated on this drawing of the boat which in 1875 took them and other Plains Indian prisoners to Jacksonville, Florida. (FIELD MUSEUM OF NATURAL HISTORY)

that they would bring all our ponies, but they only brought fifty, and the hostile Sioux came one night and stole all of them away.

In the first place, before we started from Minnesota, they told us that they had got a good country for us, where they were going to put us. The interpreter here with me now was appointed interpreter, on the first boat that came round, to see to things for the Indians on the trip round. After we got on the boat we were as though in prison. We were fed on dry stuff all the time. We started down the Mississippi River, and then up the Missouri to Dakota Territory and there we found our superintendent, and stopped there. Before we left Minnesota they told us that the superintendent had started on ahead of us, and would be there before us, and that he had plenty of Indians, and would have thirty houses built for us before we got there. After we got there they sometimes gave us rations, but not enough to go round most of the time. Some would have to go without eating two or three days.

It was not a good country. It was all dust. Whenever we cooked anything, it would be full of dust. We found out after a while we could not live there. . . . There was not enough to eat. The first winter one party started down the Missouri River as far as Fort Randall, where they wintered. Before the superintendent left us (the first fall after we went there), he had a cottonwood trough made and put beef in it, and sometimes a whole barrel of flour and a piece of pork, and let it stand a whole night, and the next morning after cooking it, would give us some of it to eat. We tried to use it, but many of us got sick on it and died. I am telling nothing but the truth now. They also put in the unwashed intestines of the beeves and the liver and lights, and, after dipping out the soup, the bottom would be very nasty and offensive. Some of the old women and children got sick on it and died. . . .

I will pass and not say more about the provision, and say of things since we left Crow Creek. For myself, in the first place, I thought I could stay there for a while and see the country. But I found out it wasn't a good country. I lost six of my children, and so I came down the Missouri River. When I got ready to start, some soldiers came there and told me if I started they would fire at me. I had thirty canoes ready to start. No one interceded with the soldiers to permit me to go. But the next night I got away and started down the river, and when I got as far as the town of Yankton, I found a man there and got some provisions, then came on down further and got more provisions of the military authorities and then went on to the Omahas. After we got to the Omahas, somebody gave me a sack of flour, and someone told us to go to the other side of the Missouri and camp, and we did so. We thought we would keep on down the river, but someone came and told us to stay, and we have been there ever since.

LITTLE HILL, *Winnebago*

· 5 ·

Standing Bear's Odyssey

This saga of removal, related by Standing Bear of the Ponca, represents the first Indian grievance to receive sympathetic attention nationally. In 1877, the Ponca were forced on the 500-mile journey retraced here. A third of their people died en route of disease and starvation; those who survived were left disabled. Afterward, Standing Bear told the account that follows to a disbelieving Omaha newspaperman, then repeated it to an overflow audience in an Omaha church. In the spring of 1880, he described the experience up and down the East Coast, provoking a storm of letters to Congress in protest.

Meanwhile Standing Bear's son had died in Indian Territory. Disobeying an edict against leaving the reservation without permission, the old chief carried his child's bones back to the ancestral Ponca burial grounds in Nebraska. Some time later, a Senate investigating committee confirmed the allegations in Standing Bear's account of his people's suffering. Decent acreage was given to those Ponca who wished to remain in Indian Territory. Recompense was made to those who had had their property confiscated during the removal. Standing Bear and his

followers were permitted to return to their old Nebraska home-
land. In 1908, the old chief died and was buried on a hill over-
looking the site of his birth.

We lived on our land as long as we can remember. No one knows how long ago we came there. The land was owned by our tribe as far back as memory of men goes. We were living quietly on our farms. All of a sudden one white man came. We had no idea what for. This was the inspector. He came to our tribe with Rev. Mr. Hinman. These two, with the agent, James Lawrence, they made our trouble.

They said the President told us to pack up—that we must move to the Indian Territory.

The inspector said to us: "The President says you must sell this land. He will buy it and pay you the money, and give you new land in the Indian Territory."

We said to him: "We do not know your authority. You have no right to move us till we have had council with the President."

We said to him: "When two persons wish to make a bargain, they can talk together and find out what each wants, and then make their agreement."

We said to him: "We do not wish to go. When a man owns anything, he does not let it go till he has received payment for it."

We said to him: "We will see the President first."

He said to us: "I will take you to see the new land. If you like it, then you can see the President, and tell him so. If not, then you can see him and tell him so." And he took all ten of our chiefs down. I went, and Bright Eyes' uncle went. He took us to look at three different pieces of land. He said we must take one of the three pieces, so the President said. After he took us down there, he said: "No pay for the land you left."

Standing Bear.

We said to him: "You have forgotten what you said before we started. You said we should have pay for our land. Now you say not. You told us then you were speaking truth."

All these three men took us down there. The man got very angry. He tried to compel us to take one of the three pieces of land. He told us to be brave. He said to us: "If you do not accept these, I will leave you here alone. You are one thousand miles from home. You have no money. You have no interpreter, and you cannot speak the language." And he went out and slammed the door. The man talked to us from long before sundown till it was nine o'clock at night.

We said to him: "We do not like this land. We could not support ourselves. The water is bad. Now send us to Washington, to tell the President, as you promised."

He said to us: "The President did not tell me to take you to Washington; neither did he tell me to take you home."

We said to him: "You have the Indian money you took to bring us down here. That money belongs to us. We would like to have some of it. People do not give away food for nothing. We must have money to buy food on the road."

He said to us: "I will not give you a cent."

We said to him: "We are in a strange country. We cannot find our way home. Give us a pass, that people may show us our way."

He said: "I will not give you any."

We said to him: "This interpreter is ours. We pay him. Let him go with us."

He said: "You shall not have the interpreter. He is mine, and not yours."

We said to him: "Take us at least to the railroad; show us the way to that."

And he would not. He left us right there. It was winter. We

started for home on foot. At night we slept in haystacks. We barely lived till morning, it was so cold. We had nothing but our blankets. We took the ears of corn that had dried in the fields; we ate it raw. The soles of our moccasins wore out. We went barefoot in the snow. We were nearly dead when we reached the Otoe Reserve. It had been fifty days. We stayed there ten days to strengthen up, and the Otoes gave each of us a pony. The agent of the Otoes told us he had received a telegram from the inspector, saying that the Indian chiefs had run away; not to give us food or shelter, or help in any way. The agent said: "I would like to understand. Tell me all that has happened. Tell me the truth. . . ."

Then we told our story to the agent and to the Otoe chiefs—how we had been left down there to find our way.

The agent said: "I can hardly believe it possible that anyone could have treated you so. The inspector was a poor man to have done this. If I had taken chiefs in this way, I would have brought them home; I could not have left them there."

In seven days we reached the Omaha Reservation. Then we sent a telegram to the President; asked him if he had authorized this thing. We waited three days for the answer. No answer came.

In four days we reached our own home. We found the inspector there. While we were gone, he had come to our people and told them to move.

Our people said: "Where are our chiefs? What have you done with them? Why have you not brought them back? We will not move till our chiefs come back."

Then the inspector told them: "Tomorrow you must be ready to move. If you are not ready you will be shot." Then the soldiers came to the doors with their bayonets, and ten families were frightened. The soldiers brought wagons; they put their things in and were carried away. The rest of the tribe would not move. . . .

Then, when he found that we would not go, he wrote for more soldiers to come.

Then the soldiers came, and we locked our doors, and the women and children hid in the woods. Then the soldiers drove all the people [to] the other side of the river, all but my brother Big Snake and I. We did not go; and the soldiers took us and carried us away to a fort and put us in jail. There were eight officers who held council with us after we got there. The commanding officer said: "I have received four messages telling me to send my soldiers after you. Now, what have you done?"

Then we told him the whole story. Then the officer said: "You have done no wrong. The land is yours; they had no right to take it from you. Your title is good. I am here to protect the the weak, and I have no right to take you; but I am a soldier, and I have to obey orders."

He said: "I will telegraph to the President, and ask him what I shall do. We do not think these three men had any authority to treat you as they have done. When we own a piece of land, it belongs to us till we sell it and pocket the money."

Then he brought a telegram, and said he had received answer from the President. The President said he knew nothing about it.

They kept us in jail ten days. Then they carried us back to our home. The soldiers collected all the women and children together; then they called all the chiefs together in council; and then they took wagons and went round and broke open the houses. When we came back from the council, we found the women and children surrounded by a guard of soldiers.

They took our reapers, mowers, hay rakes, spades, ploughs, bedsteads, stoves, cupboards, everything we had on our farms, and put them in one large building. Then they put into the wagons such things as they could carry. We told them that we would rather die than leave our lands; but we could not help ourselves. They took us down. Many died on the road. Two of my children died. After we reached the new land, all my horses died. The water was very bad. All our cattle died; not one was left. I stayed till one hundred and fifty-eight of my people had died. Then I ran away with thirty of my people, men and women and children. Some of the children were orphans. We were three months on the road. We were weak and sick and starved. When we reached the Omaha Reserve the Omahas gave us a piece of land, and we were in a hurry to plough it and put in wheat. While we were working, the soldiers came and arrested us. Half of us were sick. We would rather have died than have been carried back; but we could not help ourselves.

STANDING BEAR, *Ponca*

THE NATION'S HOOP IS BROKEN AND SCATTERED

By the 1870's the great American frontier of trackless plains and independent Indians was almost a thing of the past. A few years ahead lay the final, decisive military campaigns that would once and for all crush the rebellious Plains tribes and the Southwestern Apache. But everywhere were appearing wire fences, railroads, towns, cattle ranches, and farms. In 1870 President Grant had been advised by his Secretary of the Interior that it would "be cheaper to feed every adult Indian now living to sleepy surfeiting during his natural life, while their children are educated to self-support by agriculture, than it would be to carry on a general Indian war for a single year."

All the battle-weary and impoverished remnant tribes had been assigned reservations, although doomed breakouts were still in the offing. A map of the United States reveals that Native Americans possessed about two hundred thousand square miles of land; non-Indians held the remaining three million. In 1871 Congress passed the law forbidding the negotiation of any further Indian treaties, killing whatever hopes tribes might have had for recog-

In the 1860's and 70's the slaughter of buffalo by professional hunters spelled disaster for Plains Indians. At this Dodge City, Kansas, depot, 40,000 buffalo hides have been collected by one shipper alone, the meat left uneaten on the Plains. (KANSAS HISTORICAL SOCIETY)

nition as sovereign nations. In 1871, too, General Philip Sheridan, in charge of all Plains troops, forbade Indians to leave their western reservations without a pass from their civilian agents.

Some warriors defied the new restrictions. The year 1871 saw two aging Kiowa war chiefs, Sitting Bear and White Bear, slip away from their reservation for a last attack on white settlements in Texas. Captured, the seventy-year-old Sitting Bear sang his death song in final defiance: "O Sun, you remain forever, but we of the Ten Bravest must die. O Earth, you remain forever, but we of the Ten Bravest must die." Then, gnawing at his wrists to slip free of his handcuffs, he grabbed an empty carbine and had himself shot to death. White Bear endured confinement in Texas State Penitentiary for eight years. Then he, too, sang his death song and committed suicide by hurling himself from the prison hospital's roof.

In the latter half of the nineteenth century, a number of western tribes were gripped by a religious fervor. Native prophets like Smoholla of Oregon, Keeps His Name Always of the Southwestern Plains, and Tovaibo and his son Wovoka of the Nevada Paiute preached the same message: dance this dance as intensely as you can, and the white man will disappear. You will have visions of your ancestors; dead Indians will return to life; and buffalo will graze over the Plains once more. But on December 29, 1890, along Wounded Knee Creek in South Dakota, more than two hundred Sioux adherents of the most influential of these religious movements—the Ghost Dance—were massacred by United States troops. (As with most officially suppressed Indian rituals, the Ghost Dance only went underground. In various forms it is still practiced today by tribes in Oklahoma and California.) To many tribal elders, the time of which Black Hawk had prophesied seemed to be at hand, when Indians "would become like white men, so you can't trust them, and there must be, as in white settlements, nearly as many officers as men, to take care of them and keep them in order."

In the closing years of the nineteenth century, the vanquished Indians in the United States, fewer than 250,000 of them left, sank into anonymity on their neglected reservations. The American public would forget them, remember them, then forget them again. Native Americans would grow accustomed to being in and out of fashion. Forbidden to hunt outside reservation confines, the western tribes barely survived on humiliating handouts of government "annuities"—bad food and thin blankets for which they often had to beg. Their lives were controlled by government agents frequently in league with corrupt suppliers. They were grossly overcharged for goods that had originally been established through treaty as the Indians' due. At faraway government boarding schools run by strict clergymen or ex-army officers, Native American children were forcibly indoctrinated into the white man's ways. Many of the Indians' sacred ceremonies were banned. As the old-time chiefs and councils no longer exercised meaningful authority, the traditional tribal social structure weakened. The young were left without models, and some came to doubt the power of their forefathers' religions. As the following selections reflect, it was a time of despair over present conditions and nostalgia for past happiness.

But even at his lowest point, the Native American's sense of his own traditional identity, and his search for new forms of tribalism, were not destroyed. In the Indian "melting pot" of Oklahoma, where so many refugee tribes were well along in learning to live together, new customs, new religions, and a new political sense had emerged. In 1870, representatives of thirty-four tribes met at a council house at Okmulgee, Oklahoma, to draft a constitution for a proposed all-Indian state. Though the movement died after eight years of annual meetings, Oklahoma

Indians would remain in the vanguard of the drive for Indian self-government. In the East, most indigenous tribes had either ended up on reservations out west or blended into the surrounding population (although in the late 1960's Americans were amazed at the number of "extinct" Indians who suddenly began re-organizing as tribes along the Northeast coast). Yet the New York Iroquois, thanks to an early nineteenth-century visionary named Handsome Lake, had survived cultural disintegration and emerged stronger than ever. The strict code of Handsome Lake's "Longhouse Religion" frowned on drinking and upheld the strength of family life. A shrewd amalgam of Christian and old-time Iroquois values, the Handsome Lake movement kept the Iroquois strongly united as a traditional people right through the twentieth century.

In the Southwest, after their traumatic exile at Fort Sumner, the Navajo started a remarkable recovery as shepherds and farmers. Their neighbors, the Chiricahua Apache, were not fully subdued until the 1880's; for their more hostile bands, adjustment to white society occurred behind prison walls in the Deep South. Since no one coveted their mesa deserts, the way of life of the Pueblo Indians remained relatively unchanged. Most of their seventeenth-century land grants from Spain became their official reservations. Although Pueblo ceremonies and political structures would periodically come under government attack, these city-states remained the most "traditional" in the entire Indian world. On the other hand, a patchwork of new reservations—generally on the poorest land and ranging from two acres to twenty-five hundred—had to be created for the Californian Indian peoples who had barely survived all attempts in the nineteenth century to extinguish them.

Within this widely scattered network of communities, far from the white man's meddling ways, Native Americans entered into a time of repair and reflection. Often poor and hungry, ill housed and defenseless against disease, they nonetheless developed a resistance more in keeping with their inner resources. Never very good at conducting long-term military operations against the white invaders, many of them now found the strength for passive noncooperation. The old Crow and Blackfoot warriors, as well as their sons, balked at tilling the soil, and quietly slipped into the wilderness on four-day fasts in search of spirit protectors, undergoing self-torture to strengthen their prayers. The Kwakiutl and Tlingit of the Northwest Coast held their "Potlatch" giveaway ceremonies in private, defying the Canadian government's ban. The Hopi hid their children in corncribs rather than send them to school. The descendants of those Cherokees who had hidden in the Great Smokies, rather than suffer removal to Oklahoma, lied to the census takers who visited their log cabins. Despite severe internal factionalism over whether to follow white ways or their own, despite physical suffering and insults to their age-old beliefs, Native Americans survived the difficult decades at the turn of the twentieth century. They would reemerge into the public eye a half century later, calling once again for justice and cultural freedom. Meanwhile they survived.

And the traditionalists among them, elders like the Oglala Sioux holy man, Black Elk, kept the fires alive for a future revitalization of the Native American spirit.

"Again, and maybe for the last time on this earth," Black Elk prayed to the Great Spirit, "I recall the great vision that you sent me. It may be that some little root of the sacred tree still lives. Nourish it then, that it may leaf and bloom and fill with singing birds. Hear me, not for myself, but for my people; I am old. Hear me that they may once more go back into the sacred hoop and find the good red road, the shielding tree. In sorrow

I am sending a feeble voice, O Six Powers of the World. Hear me in my sorrow, for I may never call again. O make my people live."

· 1 ·

The Buffalo Go

In the mid-nineteenth century, professional hunters severely thinned the herds of buffalo on the Great Plains; a single hunter might kill as many as 150 animals a day. Carriage owners in the East had developed a rage for buffalo hide as lap robes, and smoked buffalo tongue had become a delicacy. To Indian hunters the near extinction of the buffalo meant the disappearance of their way of life, as a Kiowa woman named Old Lady Horse tells in this folktale.

Everything the Kiowas had came from the buffalo. Their tipis were made of buffalo hides, so were their clothes and moccasins. They ate buffalo meat. Their containers were made of hide, or of bladders or stomachs. The buffalo were the life of the Kiowas.

Most of all, the buffalo was part of the Kiowa religion. A white buffalo calf must be sacrificed in the Sun Dance. The priests used parts of the buffalo to make their prayers when they healed people or when they sang to the powers above.

So, when the white men wanted to build railroads, or when they wanted to farm or raise cattle, the buffalo still protected the Kiowas. They tore up the railroad tracks and the gardens. They chased the cattle off the ranges. The buffalo loved their people as much as the Kiowas loved them.

There was war between the buffalo and the white men. The

white men built forts in the Kiowa country, and the woolly-headed buffalo soldiers [the Tenth Cavalry, made up of black troops] shot the buffalo as fast as they could, but the buffalo kept coming on, coming on, even into the post cemetery at Fort Sill. Soldiers were not enough to hold them back.

Then the white men hired hunters to do nothing but kill the buffalo. Up and down the plains those men ranged, shooting sometimes as many as a hundred buffalo a day. Behind them came the skinners with their wagons. They piled the hides and bones into the wagons until they were full, and then took their loads to the new railroad stations that were being built, to be shipped east to the market. Sometimes there would be a pile of bones as high as a man, stretching a mile along the railroad track.

The buffalo saw that their day was over. They could protect their people no longer. Sadly, the last remnant of the great herd gathered in council, and decided what they would do.

The Kiowas were camped on the north side of Mount Scott, those of them who were still free to camp. One young woman got up very early in the morning. The dawn mist was still rising from Medicine Creek, and as she looked across the water, peering through the haze, she saw the last buffalo herd appear like a spirit dream.

Straight to Mount Scott the leader of the herd walked. Behind him came the cows and their calves, and the few young males who had survived. As the woman watched, the face of the mountain opened.

Inside Mount Scott the world was green and fresh, as it had been when she was a small girl. The rivers ran clear, not red. The wild plums were in blossom, chasing the red buds up the inside slopes. Into this world of beauty the buffalo walked, never to be seen again.

OLD LADY HORSE, *Kiowa*

· 2 ·

Take Care of Me

Upon his surrender to United States Army officers in 1858, the Seminole chief Wild Cat (Coacoochee) demanded spoils from the victors.

When I was a boy, I saw the white man afar off, and was told that he was my enemy. I could not shoot him as I would a wolf or a bear, yet he came upon me. My horse and fields he took from me. He said he was my friend—He gave me his hand in friendship; I took it, he had a snake in the other; his tongue was forked; he lied and stung me. I asked for but a small piece of this land, enough to plant and live on far to the south—a spot where I could place the ashes of my kindred—a place where my wife and child could live. This was not granted me. I am about to leave Florida forever and have done nothing to disgrace it. It was my home; I loved it, and to leave it is like burying my wife and child. I have thrown away my rifle and have taken the hand of the white man, and now I say take care of me!

WILD CAT, *Seminole*

· 3 ·

I Am Alone

During a truce talk in 1866 with General Gordon Granger, the famous Chiricahua Apache chief Cochise made this moving request to remain in Arizona's Dragoon Mountains rather than be forced to live on the Tularosa Reservation. Granger agreed, but a few months later, Cochise and his followers were ordered to move to Tularosa; they refused and resumed hostilities for another six years. After he died in 1874, Cochise was secretly buried in his old Dragoon Mountains hideout, known thereafter as Cochise Stronghold.

The sun has been very hot on my head and made me as in a fire; my blood was on fire, but now I have come into this valley and drunk of these waters and washed myself in them and they have cooled me. Now that I am cool I have come with my hands open to you to live in peace with you. I speak straight and do not wish to deceive or be deceived. I want a good, strong and lasting peace.

When God made the world he gave one part to the white man and another to the Apache. Why was it? Why did they come together? Now that I am to speak, the sun, the moon, the earth, the air, the waters, the birds and beasts, even the children unborn shall rejoice at my words. The white people have looked for me long. I am here! What do they want? They have looked for me long; why am I worth so much? If I am worth so much why not mark when I set my foot and look when I spit? The coyotes go about at night to rob and kill; I can not see them; I am not God. I am no longer chief of all the Apaches. I am no longer rich; I am but a poor man. The world was not always this way. I can not command the animals; if I would they would not obey me. God made us not as you; we were born like the animals, in the dry grass, not on beds like you. This is why we do as the animals, go about of a night and rob and steal. If I had such things as you have, I would not do as I do, for then I would not need to do so. There are Indians who go about killing and robbing. I do not

"Dangerous" war chiefs were kept under government surveillance until they died. Here is Geronimo (on the cannon) at Fort Pickens, Florida, with fellow Chiricahuas, Nachise (center) and Mangus.

command them. If I did, they would not do so. My warriors have been killed in Sonora. I came in here because God told me to do so. He said it was good to be at peace—so I came! I was going around the world with the clouds, and the air, when God spoke to my thought and told me to come in here and be at peace with all. He said the world was for us all; how was it?

When I was young I walked all over this country, east and west, and saw no other people than the Apaches. After many summers I walked again and found another race of people had come to take it. How is it? Why is it that the Apaches wait to die—that they carry their lives on their finger nails? They roam over the hills and plains and want the heavens to fall on them. The Apaches were once a great nation; they are now but few, and because of this they want to die and so carry their lives on their finger nails. Many have been killed in battle. You must speak straight so that your words may go as sunlight to our hearts. *Tell me, if the Virgin Mary has walked throughout all the land, why has she never entered the wigwam of the Apache? Why have we never seen or heard her?*

I have no father nor mother; I am alone in the world. No one cares for Cochise; that is why I do not care to live, and wish the rocks to fall on me and cover me up. If I had a father and a mother like you, I would be with them and they with me. When I was going around the world, all were asking for Cochise. Now he is here—you see him and hear him—are you glad? If so, say so. Speak, Americans and Mexicans, I do not wish to hide anything from you nor have you hide anything from me; I will not lie to you; do not lie to me. I want to live in these mountains; I do not want to go to Tularosa. That is a long ways off. The flies on those mountains eat out the eyes of the horses. The bad spirits live there. I have drunk of these waters and they have cooled me; I do not want to leave here.

COCHISE, *Chiricahua Apache*

· 4 ·

I Have Spoken

Crazy Horse, the great Oglala Sioux leader and hero of the Battle of the Little Big Horn, never had his photograph taken, and was on his deathbed before his thoughts were ever recorded on paper. Bayoneted by a Sioux guard at Fort Robinson, Nebraska, in 1877, he spoke these final words to Agent Jesse M. Lee.

My friend, I do not blame you for this. Had I listened to you this trouble would not have happened to me. I was not hostile to the white man. Sometimes my young men would attack the Indians who were their enemies and took their ponies. They did it in return.

We had buffalo for food, and their hides for clothing and our teepees. We preferred hunting to a life of idleness on the reservations, where we were driven against our will. At times we did not get enough to eat, and we were not allowed to leave the reservation to hunt.

We preferred our own way of living. We were no expense to the government then. All we wanted was peace and to be left alone. Soldiers were sent out in the winter, who destroyed our villages. Then "Long Hair" [Custer] came in the same way. They say we massacred him, but he would have done the same to us had we not defended ourselves and fought to the last. Our first impulse was to escape with our squaws and papooses, but we were so hemmed in that we had to fight.

After that I went up on Tongue River with a few of my people and lived in peace. But the government would not let me alone. Finally, I came back to the Red Cloud Agency. . . . I came here with the agent [Lee] to talk with Big White Chief, but was not given a chance. They tried to confine me, I tried to escape, and a soldier ran his bayonet into me.

I have spoken.

CRAZY HORSE, *Oglala Sioux*

· 5 ·

I Want to Look for My Children

Just thirty miles from the Canadian border and the freedom he prized so dearly, Chief Joseph and his band of Nez Percé fugitives were finally caught by Colonel Nelson Miles and General O. O. Howard. On October 5, 1877, Chief Joseph made his now famous surrender statement.

Old enemies meet in 1904: the Nez Percé chief, Joseph, and the general who pursued him to within sight of freedom in Canada, O. O. Howard.
(NEBRASKA HISTORICAL SOCIETY)

Tell General Howard I know his heart. What he told me before, I have in my heart.

I am tired of fighting. Our chiefs are killed. Looking Glass is dead. Toohoolhoolzote is dead. The old men are all dead.

It is the young men who say yes and no. He who led on the young men is dead. It is cold and we have no blankets. The little children are freezing to death.

My people, some of them, have run away to the hills, and have no blankets, no food; no one knows where they are—perhaps freezing to death.

I want to have time to look for my children and see how many I can find. Maybe I shall find them among the dead.

Hear me, my chiefs. I am tired; my heart is sick and sad.

From where the sun now stands I will fight no more forever.

CHIEF JOSEPH, *Nez Percé*

· 6 ·

No Dawn to the East

To one tribal elder, the end of the Indian world as he had known it felt like this.

My sun is set. My day is done. Darkness is stealing over me. Before I lie down to rise no more I will speak to my people. Hear me, for this is not the time to tell a lie. The Great Spirit made us, and gave us this land we live in. He gave us the buffalo, antelope, and deer for food and clothing. Our hunting grounds stretched from the Mississippi to the great mountains.

We were free as the winds and heard no man's commands. We fought our enemies, and feasted our friends. Our braves drove away all who would take our game. They captured women and horses from our foes. Our children were many and our herds were large. Our old men talked with spirits and made good medicine. Our young men hunted and made love to the girls. Where the tipi was, there we stayed, and no house imprisoned us. No one said, "To this line is my land, to that is yours." Then the white man came to our hunting grounds, a stranger. We gave him meat and presents, and told him go in peace. He looked on our women and stayed to live in our tipis. His fellows came to build their roads across our hunting grounds. He brought among us the mysterious iron that shoots. He brought with him the magic water that makes men foolish. With his trinkets and beads he even bought the girl I loved. I said, "The white man is not a friend, let us kill him." But their numbers were greater than blades of grass. They took away the buffalo and shot down our best warriors. They took away our lands and surrounded us by fences. Their soldiers camped outside with cannon to shoot us down. They wiped the trails of our people from the face of the prairies. They forced our children to forsake the ways of their fathers. When I turn to the east I see no dawn. When I turn to the west the approaching night hides all.

ANONYMOUS, *Tribe unknown*

· 7 ·

Gone Forever

In the mid-nineteenth century, when she was a child, Buffalo Bird Woman of the Hidatsa tribe lived along a bend of the

Buffalo Bird Woman in 1926. (STATE HISTORICAL SOCIETY OF NORTH DAKOTA)

Missouri River named "Like a Fishhook." As an old woman she looks back on those faraway times.

I am an old woman now. The buffaloes and black-tail deer are gone, and our Indian ways are almost gone. Sometimes I find it hard to believe that I ever lived them.

My little son grew up in the white man's school. He can read books, and he owns cattle and has a farm. He is a leader among our Hidatsa people, helping teach them to follow the white man's road.

He is kind to me. We no longer live in an earth lodge, but in a house with chimneys; and my son's wife cooks by a stove.

But for me, I cannot forget our old ways.

Often in summer I rise at daybreak and steal out to the cornfields; and as I hoe the corn I sing to it, as we did when I was young. No one cares for our corn songs now.

Sometimes at evening I sit, looking out on the big Missouri. The sun sets, and dusk steals over the water. In the shadows I seem again to see our Indian village, with smoke curling upward from the earth lodges; and in the river's roar I hear the yells of the warriors, the laughter of little children as of old. It is but an old woman's dream. Again I see but shadows and hear only the roar of the river; and tears come into my eyes. Our Indian life, I know, is gone forever.

BUFFALO BIRD WOMAN, *Hidatsa*

· 8 ·

This Awful Loneliness

These are the words of an old Omaha tribesman remembering the landscape as he and his people had once known it along the western bank of the Missouri River, between the Platte and Niobrara rivers, in present-day Nebraska.

When I was a youth, the country was very beautiful. Along the rivers were belts of timberland, where grew cottonwood, maple, elm, ash, hickory, and walnut trees, and many other kinds. Also there were many kinds of vines and shrubs. And under these grew many good herbs and beautiful flowering plants.

In both the woodland and the prairie I could see the trails of many kinds of animals and could hear the cheerful songs of many kinds of birds. When I walked abroad, I could see many forms of life, beautiful living creatures which *Wakanda* [the Great Spirit] had placed here; and these were, after their manner, walking, flying, leaping, running, playing all about.

But now the face of all the land is changed and sad. The living creatures are gone. I see the land desolate and I suffer an unspeakable sadness. Sometimes I wake in the night, and I feel as though I should suffocate from the pressure of this awful feeling of loneliness.

ANONYMOUS, *Omaha*

· 9 ·
A Wish

The virtual extinction of the buffalo on the northern Plains was directly responsible for the death by starvation of some six hundred Blackfoot Indians in the winter of 1883–84. Before he himself died during that "Starvation Winter," a Blackfoot named Flint Knife expressed this thought.

I wish that white people had never come into my country.

FLINT KNIFE, *Blackfoot*

NOTES ON SOURCES

Beginning with Charles Hamilton's *Cry of the Thunderbird: The Indian's Own Story* (Macmillan, 1950), a growing number of modern anthologies have offered Native American accounts and interpretations of Indian and white relations. My documentary differs mainly in its tighter, chronological focus on the central themes of this long history. It also benefits from the surprising quantity of Indian oral tradition exhumed each year from the archives.

The publication in 1825 of *A Memoir of Catherine Brown, A Christian Indian of the Cherokee Nation* inaugurated a primary source for these later anthologies: the Indian's own story. From then until the early part of the twentieth century, American Indian life histories were put into print by journalists and offbeat historians. Then in 1913, the trained anthropologist Paul Radin published his landmark *Personal Reminiscences of a Winnebago Indian* in the *Journal of American Folklore*. Now scholars familiar with the cultural background of their subjects became co-authors in life histories which, with greater intimacy and authenticity, brought home to non-Indians the inner workings of tribal life.

Anthologists like myself can also draw from an array of eighteenth- and nineteenth-century Indian speeches, collected by such nineteenth-century writers as Samuel G. Drake and B. B. Thatcher. Usually overheard during formal discussions between chiefs and white officials, this body of "Indian oratory" reinforced the romantic image of the red man as noble savage (a view that was as unrealistic as that which saw him as bloodthirsty savage). Many of these speeches were dressed up by interpreters and transcribers with flowery, decorative figures of speech and oratorical devices; the result is that the speeches bear little resemblance to anything that ever came out of an Indian's mouth. I have used them only when the basic statement rings true.

Library collections of Indian oral materials include the Ayer Room at the Newberry Library, Chicago, and the six regional centers of the Doris Duke Indian Oral History Project. The latter, an ambitious, privately funded project, enabled scholars around the country to interview tribal elders from 1967 to 1972. The resulting tapes and their transcriptions have supplied material for two anthologies, *To Be An Indian* (Cash and Hoover, 1971) and *The Zuñi: Self-Portrayals* (The Zuñi People, 1972).

But most Indian-uttered accounts have to be ferreted out of the nooks and crannies of white history and scholarship. One must plow through official transcripts of the proceedings of treaty councils and of testimony before Congress, read state historical-society quarterlies, the works of frontier journalists, and the memoirs of old military officers, and one must rediscover the writings of nineteenth-century, college-educated Indians, and especially resurrect the works of the pioneer anthropologists, linguists, and folklorists. Such research is haphazard prospecting, and sometimes turns up only fool's gold. The most blatant example recently was the 1972 publication of *Memoirs of Chief Red Fox*, the life of a "Sioux Chief" that continued to sell in the thousands even after the authenticity of the text was challenged.

Luckily some good bibliographies now exist to guide interested students to many of the buried gems of Indian oral tradition. *American Indian and Eskimo Authors*, compiled by Arlene B. Hirschfelder (Association on American Indian Affairs, 1973), *Indian-Inuit Authors; An Annotated Bibliography* (National Library of Canada, 1974), and *The Indians and Eskimos of North America: A Bibliography of Books in Print through 1972*, compiled by Jack W. Marken (Dakota Press, 1973), are three useful general directories. Covering most of the Indian autobiographical literature are L. L. Langness's *The Life History in Anthropological Science* (Holt, 1965) and Louis R. Gottschalk's *The Use of Personal Documents in History, Anthropology and Sociology* (1949). The Association for the Study of American Indian Literature at Columbia University's Department of English, New York City, has recently established a *Newsletter*, which serves as a valuable clearinghouse for work on oral tradition as well as contemporary Indian writing.

One final remark: the usefulness of oral tradition to objective, formal history has been debated ever since the anthropologist Robert Lowie in 1915 criticized Dr. John Swanton's article on "Primitive American History" with the remark, "When we find, for instance, that in an Assiniboine creation myth, the trickster-hero makes the earth, regulates the seasons, and created men and horses in practically a single breath . . . we may well be skeptical as to historical reconstructions from native accounts." I, however, have been less interested in whether a selection constitutes a precise historical reconstruction of an event than in what it reflects of how Native Americans experienced that event.

The unrecognized partners in such a project are the librarians and archivists who have helped me track down the materials, as well as the friends who have pointed me to sources and read what I came up with: John Aubrey of the Newberry Library, Chicago; Leslie Navari, Pacific Grove Library, Pacific Grove; Monterey Peninsula College Library, Monterey; Museum of the American Indian Research Facility, New York; University of Maine Special Collections, Orono; Bancroft Library and Lowie Library of Anthropology, Berkeley; Mike Cowdry; Dr. Ray Fogelson; Patrocinia Gonzales; Valerie Kack; Clyde Milner; Arnold Seibel. Special thanks go to Roy Clausen, Howard McFann and Abbie Lou Williams for enabling my research.

PREMONITIONS AND PROPHECIES

1. "He Will Use Any Means to Get What He Wants" from *The Great Resistance: A Hopi Anthology* edited by George Yamada. Privately printed, March, 1957.

2. "White Rabbit Got Lotsa Everything" from "Out of the Past: A True Indian Story" told by Lucy Young to Edith V. A. Murphey. *California Historical Society Quarterly*, Vol. XX, No. 4 (December, 1941).

3. "Visitors from Heaven" from *Legends of My People: The Great Ojibway* by Norval Morriseau, edited by Selwyn Dewdney. Toronto: Ryerson Press, 1965.

4. "Thunder's Dream Comes True" from *Life of Ma-Ka-Tai-Me-She-Kia-Kiak or Black Hawk* dictated by himself. Cincinnati, 1833. Available as *Black Hawk: An Autobiography* edited by Donald Jackson. Urbana: University of Illinois Press, 1964.

5. "Easy Life of the Gray-Eyed" from *Flaming Arrow's People* by James Paytiamo. New York: Duffield, Duffield and Green, 1932.

6. "The Spider's Web" from *Black Elk Speaks* by John G. Neihardt. Lincoln: University of Nebraska Press, 1961.

FACE TO FACE

1. "Their Wondrous Works and Ways" from *Indian Boyhood* by Charles A. Eastman. New York: McClure, Philips and Co., 1902.

2. "Before They Got Thick" from "The White People Who Came In A Boat" by M. E. Opler. *Memoirs of the American Folklore Society*, Vol. XXXVI, 1940.

3. "Silmoodawa Gives a Complete Performance" from *Legends of the Micmacs* by Silas Tertius Rand. New York and London: Longmans, Green and Co., 1894.

4. "A Different Kind of Man" from *The Assiniboines: From the Accounts of the Old Ones Told to First Boy (James Larpenteur Long)*, edited and with an Introduction by Michael Stephen Kennedy. Norman: University of Oklahoma Press, 1961.

5. "I Hid Myself and Watched": Part one (Pretty Shield) from *Red Mother* by Frank Bird Linderman. New York: John Day and Co., 1932. Part two (Jaime) from *The Navaho Door: An Introduction to Navaho Life* by Alexander Leighton and Dorothea Leighton. Cambridge: Harvard University Press, 1944.

EXCHANGE BETWEEN WORLDS

1. "Thunder, Dizzying Liquid, and Cups That Do Not Grow" from *The Menominee Indians* by Walter James Hoffman. 14th Annual Report, Part 1. Washington, D.C.: Smithsonian Institution Bureau of Ethnology, 1896 (1897).

2. "Keep Your Presents" from *Pawnee Hero Stories and Folk Tales* by George Bird Grinnell. New York, 1889.

3. "Give Us Good Goods" from *Isham's Observations and Notes 1743–49*. London: *Hudson's Bay Record Society*, Volume XII, 1949.

4. "You Rot the Guts of Our Young Men" from *North Carolina Colonial Records*, Volume 5. Chapel Hill: University of North Carolina.

5. "Some Strange Animal" from *Story of the Indian* by George Bird Grinnell. New York: Appleton Publishing Co., 1895.

6. "Buttocks Bags and Green Coffee Bread" from "Rations" by M. E. Opler. *Memoirs of the American Folklore Society*, Vol. XXXI, 1938.

7. "The Bewitched Pale Man" from "Tales from the Dogribs" by June Helm and Vital Thomas. *The Beaver Magazine*, Hudson's Bay Co., Autumn, 1966.

BEARERS OF THE CROSS

1. "Burn the Temples, Break Up the Bells" from *Revolt of the Pueblo Indians of New Mexico and Otermin's Attempted Reconquest 1680–1682* by Charles Wilson Hackett. Albuquerque: University of New Mexico Press, 1942.

2. "A Good Indian's Dilemma" from *Being a Mesquakie Indian* by Lisa Redfield Peattie. Chicago: University of Chicago Press, 1950.

3. "We Never Quarrel About Religion" from *Indian Biography* by B. B. Thatcher. New York, 1845.

4. "Janitin Is Named *Jésus*" "Testimonio de Janitil" from "*Apuntes Historicos de la Baja California*" by Manuel C. Roja. Berkeley: Bancroft Library (Mss. #295).

5. "The Freedom to Work" from *Indian Life and Customs at Mission San Luis Rey* by Pablo Tac, edited and translated and with a historical introduction by Minna and Gordon Hewes. California: Old Mission San Luis Rey, 1958.

6. "A Shaman Obeys" from "The Language of the Salinan Indians" by J. Alden Mason. *Publications in American Archeology and Ethnology*, Volume 14, No. 1. Berkeley: University of California Publications, 1918.

7. "Always Give Blessings and Be Thankful" from *Jim Whitewolf: The Life of a Kiowa Apache Indian* with an introduction and epilogue by Charles S. Brant. New York: Dover Publications, Inc., 1969.

LIVING BESIDE EACH OTHER

1. "Remove the Cause of Our Uneasiness" from *Biography and History of the Indians of North America* by Samuel G. Drake. Boston, 1841.

2. "Mary Jemison Becomes an Iroquois" from *A Narrative of the Life of Mrs. Mary Jemison* by James Everett Seaver. New York: J. D. Bemis and Co., 1824.

3. "Our Very Good Friend Kirk" from *Letter Book of the Indian Agency at Fort Wayne 1809–1815* edited by Gayle Thornbrough. Indianapolis: Indiana Historical Society, 1961.

4. "The Frenchman Dreams Himself Home" from *The Winnebago Tribe* by Paul Radin. Thirty-Seventh Annual Report. Smithsonian Institution Bureau of Ethnology. Washington: Government Printing Office, 1923.

5. "Incident at Boyer Creek" from *The Omaha Language* by J. O. Dorsey. Contributions to North American Ethnology, Department of the Interior, United States Geographical and Geological Survey of the Rocky Mountain Region, V. VI, Washington, 1890.

6. "If I Could See This Thing" from *Life of George Bent: Written From His Letters* by George Hyde, edited by Savoie Lottinville. Norman: University of Oklahoma Press, 1968.

7. "All Things Are Connected" from a letter written in 1855 by the Dwanish Chief Seattle to President Franklin Pierce. Released by U.S. Government in 1976.

THE LONG RESISTANCE

1. "We Must Be United" from *Memoirs of a Captivity Among the Indians of North America* by John D. Hunter. London, 1924.

2. "Black Hawk Stands Alone" from "Black-Hawk War" by William Jones. *Journal of American Folklore*, 24:235–27, 1911.

3. "Blood Scattered like Water" from "The Stone and Kelsey 'Massacre' on the Shores of Clear Lake in 1849, The Indian Viewpoint." *California Historical Society Quarterly*, XI, No. 3, (September, 1932).

4. "Young Men, Go Out and Fight Them" from *Wooden Leg: A Warrior Who Fought Custer*, interpreted by Thomas B. Marquis. Lincoln: University of Nebraska Press, 1962.

5. "Geronimo Puts Down the Gun" from *I Fought With Geronimo* by Jason Betzinez with Wilbur Sturtevant Nye. Harrisburg: Stackpole Company, 1959.

THE TREATY TRAIL

1. "Let Us Examine the Facts" from *Tatham's Characters Among The North American Indians*. Annual of Biography and Obituary. London, 1820.

2. "Osceola Determined" from *The War In Florida: Being An Exposition of Its Causes* by Woodburne Potter. Baltimore: Lewis and Coleman, 1836.

3. "My Son, Stop Your Ears" from "An Indian's View of Indian Affairs." *North American Review*, CCLXIX (April, 1879).

4. "We Are Not Children" from U. S. National Archives, Office of Indian Affairs. Letters Sent: Otoe Agency (1856–1876).

5. "Plenty Coups Travels to Washington" from the unpublished manuscript "A Crow Miscellany" by William Wildschut. New York Museum of the American Indian, Heye Foundation.

EXILES IN THEIR OWN LAND

1. "Plea from the Chickasaw" from *Journal of Chickasaw Council, October 16, 1826 to November 1, 1826.* American State Papers, Indian Affairs, Vol. II.

2. "Tushpa Crosses the Mississippi" from *The American Indian Magazine,* October-November-December, 1928, and January, 1929. Tulsa, Oklahoma.

3. "Corralling the Navajo" from *The Navajo Indians* by Dane Coolidge and Mary R. Coolidge. Boston and New York: Houghton Mifflin Co., 1930.

4. "The Uprooted Winnebago" from U.S. Senate Report No. 156, 39th Congress, 2nd Session, 1866-1867.

5. "Standing Bear's Odyssey" from *A Century of Dishonor* by Helen Hunt Jackson. Boston: Roberts Brothers, 1893.

THE NATION'S HOOP IS BROKEN AND SCATTERED

1. "The Buffalo Go" from *American Indian Mythology* by Alice Marriott and Carol K. Rachlin. New York: Thomas Y. Crowell Company, 1968.

2. "Take Care of Me" from *Broken Peace Pipes* by Irwin M. Peithman, foreword by Loren Taylor. Springfield, Ill.: Charles C. Thomas, Publisher, 1964.

3. "I Am Alone" from "Reflections of an Interview with Cochise," by A. N. Ellis, Kansas State Historical Society, Vol. 13 (1913-1914).

4. "I Have Spoken" from *Twenty Years Among Our Savage Indians* by J. Leo Humfreville. Hartford: Hartford Publishing Co., 1897.

5. "I Want to Look for My Children" from U. S. Congress, House Executive Document, 45th Congress, 2nd Session, 1877-1878.

6. "No Dawn to the East" from *Red Man's Reservations* by Clark Wissler, with a new introduction by Ralph K. Andrist. New York: The Macmillan Co., 1971.

7. "Gone Forever" from *Waheenee: An Indian Girl's Story Told By Herself to Gilbert L. Wilson. North Dakota History: Journal of the Northern Plains,* 38, No. 1 & 2 (Winter/Spring, 1971).

8. "This Awful Loneliness" from *Prairie Smoke* by Melvin R. Gilmore. New York: Columbia University Press, 1929.

9. "A Wish" from *Apauk: Caller of Buffalo* by James Willard Schultz. Boston and New York: Houghton-Mifflin Co., 1915.

INDEX

(Page numbers in italics indicate illustrations.)

Abnaki, 63
Acoma, *x*, 14–15
Apache, 115, 116, 215
   Chiricahua, *92*, 139–145, *142*, 218, 222–225
   Jicarilla, 53–55
   Kiowa, *see* Kiowa
   Lipan, 26–28
   Mescalero, 27
   Warm Springs, *116*, 143
Arapaho, 78, 105, 133
Arikara, 116
Arthur, Chester, 198, 203
Assiniboine, 30–33, 133
Atkinson, Henry, 122
Aztec, 4, 29

Bad Hawk, 30–33
Bahana, 5–6
Benson, William, 125–132
Bent, George, 105–107
Betzinez, Jason, 139–145
Bigmouth, Percy, 26–28
Black Elk, 16, 17, *17*, 219–220
Blackfoot, 40, 50, 150, 219, 232
Black Hawk, 12–14, 115, 121–125, 150, 216–217
Black Hawk War, 121–125
Bloody Island Massacre (1850), 125–132
Boyer Creek incident (1853), 101–105
buffalo, slaughter of, 40, *214*, 220–221, 229, 232
Buffalo Bird Woman, 229–231, *230*
Buffalo Chief, 147
Buffalo Dance, 68
Bureau of Indian Affairs, 114–115

Cabot, John and Sebastian, 38
Canada, 4, 10–12, 13, 21, 23, 29, 40, 56–57, 63, 84, 113, 219

captivity narratives, 89–95
Caribbean, native peoples of, 19–20
Carson, Christopher "Kit," 198
Cartier, Jacques, 20, 38
Catawba, 48–49, 62
ceremonies, 60, 61, 62, 65, 67, 68, 216, 217, 219, 220
Champlain, Samuel de, 13
Cherokee, 13, 37, 114, 152–155, 160, 186–189, 219
Cheyenne, *18*, 78, 105–107, 132–139, 147
Chickasaw, 114, 161, 186, 189–191
Chinook, 38
Chippewa, 151
Choctaw, 161, 186–189, 191–197
Christianity (*see also* religion), 20, 21, 60–81, 87, 192, 218, 225
Chumash rock painting, *31*
Civilized Tribes, 186–189, 190
clothing, 53–54, 86, 96
Cochise, 227–230
Colbert, Levi, 190–191
colonial era, 21, 63, 86–87
   Indian friendship in, 87–89
   warfare in, 40, 112–114, 116–117
Columbus, Christopher, 1–4, 19, 28
Comanche, 105, 107
Corn Tassel, 152–155
Coronado, Francisco, 20, 22
Cortez, Hernando, 4, 28
Crazy Horse, 16, 133, 225–226
Cree, *36*
Creek, 62, 87, 112, 156, 157, 161, 184, 186, 188
Creek Confederacy, 3
Crimont, Father, 79
Crook, George, 140, 141
Crow, 33–35, 79, 116, 133, 176–181, *179*, 183, 219
Culberson, James, 191–197
Curly Chief, 45–47, *46*
Custer, George A., 117, 132–133, 231

Deganawida, 3
Delaware, 84, *88*, 95, 113, 114, 149, 184–185
de Soto, Hernando, 20
disease, 45, 105–107, 184, 219
Dodge, Henry Chee, 198
Dodge City depot, *214*
Dogrib, 56–57
Dorsey, J. O., 102
Dwamish, 83, 107–109

Eastman, Charles Alexander, 23–26, *24*
Encinales, Pedro, 77
English, 21–22, 38, 39, 40, 63–64, 86–87, 112–114, 115, 118, 152, 184
Eskimos, first contacts with, 22
Espejo, Antonio de, 41

farming, Indian, 41, 218
Flint Knife, 232
Fox (Mesquakie), 68, 121–125, 184
Franklin, Benjamin, 84
French, 38, 39, 40, 42, 56, 63, 84, 98–101, 112–113, 184
  Indians as viewed by, 20–21
French and Indian War, 40, 113
fur trade, 10, 21, 33, *36*, 38, 39–40, 42, 99
Fu-Sang, Kingdom of, 4

Geronimo, 139–145, *142*, *224*
Ghost Dance, 216
Gold Rush, 7, 105, 132
Granger, Gordon, 222–223
Grant, Ulysses S., 215
Grinnell, George Bird, 50
Gros Ventre, 133
guns, 38, 42, 44, 45–46, 47, 99, 115

Haglar, King, 48–49
Handsome Lake, 218
Harrison, William Henry, 118, 121, 149
Hayes, Rutherford B., 180–181
Hiawatha, 3
Hidatsa, 183, 234–236
Hopi (Moqui), 4, 5, 6, 41, 62, 200, 202, 219

horses, 41, 49–53, 111
Howard, O. O., 163, 227–228, *227*
Howling Wolf, pictures by, *18*, *205*
Hubbell, Lorenzo, trading post, *55*
Hudson, Henry, 38
Hudson's Bay Company, 10, 12, 47, 52, 56–57
hunting, 41, 49, 85, 169, 171, 180–181, *214*, 217, 220–221, 226, 228, 229
Hurons, 4, 20, 38, 40, 184

Indian Appropriation Act (1871), 150
Indian Claims Commission, 152
Indian Removal Act (1830), 187
Indian Territory, 169, *182*, 185–191, 195, 217–218
Indian-white contacts (*see also* Native Americans), 1–14, *18*, *92*
  first, 3–5, 22, 23–36, *31*
  friendship in, 83–97, *88*
  prophecies of, 4–6, 13, 14, 16–17
Iroquois, 3, 37, 40, 49, 69–70, 89–95, 114, 168, 184, 218

Jackson, Andrew, 150, 186–187
Jackson, William Henry, photograph by, *46*
Jamestown settlement, 87–89, 117
Janitin, 70–73
Jefferson, Thomas, 96–97, 185, 186
Jemison, Mary, 89–95
Jesuits, 63, 79
Johnson, Raymond, drawing by, *199*
Jolliet, Louis, 63
Jones, William, 121–125
Joseph, Chief, 150, 162–168, 227–228, *227*
Journeycake, Chief, 184–185

Kamia, 70–73
Katchongva, Dan, 5–6
Keeps His Name Always, 216
Kickapoo, 124–125
Kiowa, 22, 65, 78–81, 105, 107, *110*, 183, 216, 220–221
Kutenai, 50–51
Kwakiutl, *82*, 219

land, attitudes toward, 85–86, 87, 102, 107–108, 116
La Salle, Robert de, 21
Las Casas, Father Bartolomé de, 61
liquor, 38, 39, 41, 42, 43–44, 48–49, 123
Little Big Horn, battle of, 132–139, 225–226
Little Crow, 117
Little Hill, 203–207
Little Turtle, 117
Loa-Kum-Artnuk, 116
Long, James Larpenteur (First Boy), 30–33
Longhouse Religion, 218
Luiseño, 65, 73–76, 75

McKinn, Santiago, 92
Manifest Destiny, 87
marriage, Indian-white, 20, 21, 42, 83–84, 98–101
Marshall, John, 187
Maskegon, 56
Mather, Cotton, 63
Medicine Horse, 168–176, 169
medicine men, 10–12, 16–17, 60, 65, 66, 77
Menomini, 42–44
Mexico, Mexicans, 4, 62–63, 115, 140, 141–142, 198, 200, 201
Micmac, 28–29
Miles, Nelson, 143, 144, 232
missionaries, 61–81, 192
Mission Indians, 62–63
Monroe, James, 86
Montezuma, 4
Mormons, 101–105
Morriseau, Norval, 10–12
Mound Builders, 2
mountains, sacred, 58, 59

Naranjo, Pedro, 65–68
Narraganset, 63
Native Americans:
    cultural disintegration of, 215–218, 220–232
    cultural diversity of, 1–3
    in European courts, 28–29

pride in identity of, 86, 217–218
white pioneers aided by, 26, 28
Navajo, 33, 35, 41, 59, 115, 183, 197–203, 199, 218
Neihardt, John G., 16
New France, 21, 63
New Spain, 20, 62
Nez Percé, 150, 162–168, 227–228
Nicolet, Jean, 42
Nipissing, 38
Northwest Ordinance (1787), 149

Ojibway, 10–12
    "shaking tent" of, 11
Oklahoma, see Indian Territory
Old Lady Horse, 220–221
Old Snake, 96–97
Omaha, 101–105, 124–125, 204, 207, 211, 213, 231–232
Onondaga, 114
Opechancanough, 117
Osage, 13, 29, 116, 118, 184
Osceola, 155–162
Otoe, 168–176, 211

Paiute, 202, 216
Pawnee, 45–47, 86, 105, 116, 160
Paytiamo, James, 14, 15
Petalesharo, 86
Peyri, Father Antonio, 73–75
Philip, King, 113, 117
Piegan, 50–53
Pierce, Franklin, 107
Plains Indians, 22, 45, 49–50, 132–133, 205, 214, 215
Plenty Coups, 176–181, 179
Pomo, 38, 125–132
Ponca, 207–213
Pontiac, 113, 118
Potawatomi, 124–125, 151, 184
Powhatan Confederacy, 3, 87–89
Pretty Shield, 33–35, 34
Protestantism, 63–64
Pueblo, 14–15, 41, 62, 112, 117, 183, 197, 218
    San Felipe, 65–68
Pueblo Rebellion (1680), 62, 65–68

Quakers, *88*, 96–97
Quetzalcoatl, 4

Radin, Paul, 98
railroads, coming of, *226*
Rale, Sebastian, 63
Rand, Silas T., 29
Red Cloud, 117, 147
Red Jacket, 69–70, 168
religion, 21, 59–81
    Christian, effect of, 60–65, *64*, 68,
      71–76, 77, 78–81, 192
    Indian, 59–60, 65, 67, 68, 69–70, 77–
      81, 117, 118, 124, 216–220
    reservations, 86–87, 150, 204, 211, 213,
      215–216, 217, 218, 223, 226
    resettlement, *182*, 183–213, *199*, *205*
    U.S. policy of, 185–189
Revolutionary War, 114, 116, 149, 152
"right of discovery," 85–86
Ross, John, 187, *188*

St. Clair, Arthur, 117, 118
Salinan, 77
San Luis Rey de Francia, Mission of,
    73, 75, 76
Santee, 23–26, 133
Sauk, 12–14, 115, 121–125, 150, 184
Seattle, Chief, 83, 107, *109*
Seminole, 155–162, 184, 222
Seneca, 114
Shawnee, 96–97, 114, 118–121, 124
sheepherding, 33, 41, 218
Sheridan, Philip, 216
Shingas, Chief, 113
Shoshoni, 41, 50, 136, 138
Sioux, 4–5, 23, 41, 105, 124, 132–139,
    151, 178, 183, 204, 205
    Oglala, 16–17, 147, 219, 225–226
Sitting Bear, 216
Sitting Bull, 133
Smith, Edward P., 169–176
Smith, Captain John, 88, 89
Soaring Eagle, drawing by, *205*
Spanish, 41, 65–68, 84, 85–86, 112, 117,
    148, 197, 218
    as conquistadors, 4, 20, 22, 61

enslavement by, 19–20, 112
    as missionaries, 61–63, 70–77
Speckled Snake, Chief, 87
Standing Bear, 207–213, *209*
Standing Bear, Luther, 60

Tac, Pablo, 73–76
Taino, 19
Tecumseh, 118–121, 122, 124
Thomas, Vital, 56, 57
Thompson, Wiley, 155–162
Tlingit, 219
tobacco, 38, 43, 48, 99
Tonajinni (Blanca Peak), *58*
trading, 37–57, *36*, 99
treaties, 42, 45–46, 117, 121, 122–124,
    132, *146*, 147–181, *158*, 186, 197–
    200, 215–216
    Indian view of, 148, 150, 152–155

Ute, 41, 198, 200, 201, 202

Vikings, 4, 19, 38

Wahunsonacock, 87–89
Waioskasit, 42–44
Wampanoag, 116–117
warfare, 27, 111–145
    Indian-U.S., *110*, 112, 114–145, 156,
      216, 222–228
    intertribal, 40, 111, 112, 113, *116*,
      184, 186
Wasco Indians, 5
Washington, George, 114, 168
Weatherford, William, 112
Whitewolf, Jim, 78–81
Wild Cat (Coacoochee), 222
Williams, Roger, 63, 86
Winnebago, 98–101, 124–125, 203–207
Wintun, 5, 6
Wolf Calf, 49–53
Wooden Leg, 132–139, *134*
Wounded Knee massacre, 112, 216

Young, Lucy, 6–9, *8*

Zuñi, 22, 62, 200, 201, 202

DATE DUE